FAIRACRES PUBLICATIONS 227

AND WE SHALL BE CHANGED

Christian Reflections on Death and Dying

James Ramsay

© 2025 SLG Press
First Edition 2025

FAIRACRES PUBLICATIONS 227

ISBN 978-0-7283-0419-2
Fairacres Publications Series ISSN 0307-1405

James Ramsay asserts the right to be identified as the author of this work, in accordance with the Copyright Designs and Patents act, 1988.

All rights reserved. No part of this publication may be reproduced, stored in a retrieval system, or transmitted, in any form or by any means, electronic, mechanical, photocopying, recording or otherwise, without the prior permission of the copyright owner.

The publishers have no control over, or responsibility for, any third-party website referred to in this book. All internet addresses given in this book were correct at the time of going to press. The authors and publisher regret any inconvenience caused if addresses have changed or sites have ceased to exist, but can accept no responsibility for any such changes.

Biblical quotations are taken from the New Revised Standard Version of the Bible unless otherwise noted.

Edited and typeset in Palatino Linotype by Julia Craig-McFeely

SLG Press
Convent of the Incarnation
Fairacres • Oxford
www.slgpress.co.uk

Printed by
Grosvenor Group Ltd, Loughton, Essex

CONTENTS

Introduction	1
The Spectre Unmasked	4
Life as Story	8
'Death be not Proud'	12
Body and Soul	17
The Sanctity of the Body	24
Confronting Reality with Courage	29
Faith and Prayer in a Terminal Context	39
The Necessity of Prayer	48
Knowing We Are not Alone	58
'I Hope I'll be Alive when I Die'	69

And We Shall be Changed

INTRODUCTION

In these pages I reflect on areas of universal human experience that most of us most of the time prefer not to think about. Death in its many guises is generally an unwelcome topic of conversation. It arouses disturbing instincts, emotions and memories. When we are fit and well, it is natural to focus on living. We know, as an abstract fact, that life has a cut-off point. ... Death and the taxman are the only certainties. We might have made a will, and perhaps expressed a wish as to burial or cremation, and where we would like our ashes to be scattered or our body to be buried. But meanwhile it is important to make the most of life, and it is widely seen as morbid to dwell on our mortality.

However, while it is indeed possible to entertain a morbid preoccupation with death, and to develop a damaging anxiety about dying, it is equally possible to allow fear of death or distaste for our mortality to drive us into escapist activism in which discussion of death is taboo. This can create a disconnect from the basic realities of our existence, leading to a certain mental shallowness, emotional instability and, to use a biblical phrase, 'hardness of heart'.

Death, dying, grief and the problems thrown up by modern medical science when we do *not* die are the main themes considered here. But undergirding and overarching every discussion is the greater theme of life, and what it means in the fullest sense to live.

Christian theology and prayer offer a unique way of approaching these matters. Different currents within Christian tradition will offer different angles of approach, yet in the end it is lived encounter with the Word[1] among us, the human reality of spiritual desire and

---

[1] The opening of the Gospel of St John uses the Greek word *Logos*, the Word. In Greek *Logos* is both a thoroughly down-to-earth word and a word rich in meaning and philosophical associations, which the English 'Word' can at best hint at through use of a capital 'W'.

engagement with a greater, relational reality beyond all discussion and doctrinal constructs, that brings understanding. Statements of belief are important, but prior to these, and more fundamental, is this experience of unfathomable, inspiring and consoling relationship. Here is the heart of faith. Whether mediated primarily through participation in a Church community or through the prism of personal experience; whether tentative, faltering, doubting; struggling, confused yet persevering; confident, unapologetic and joyous—it is this unaccountable sense of relationship that brings a knowledge and appreciation of life in its transcendent immediacy that 'correct' thinking can never attain.

Theology and credal statements are too often instrumentalized: irreducible mystery conceptualized into dogmatic argument or conundrums with intellectual answers. The reflections I offer here do not attempt answers. I hope rather that they reflect the spirit of a Creed: 'We believe ... Amen,' rather than, 'We know ... QED.' The distinction being that a credo, however confident, has an element of subjectivity, of interiority, that is unacceptable to mathematical certainty.

Properly understood, theology's purpose is to strengthen us to seek and live in the light of Divine Love. When in 1273 the great Doctor of the Church St Thomas Aquinas received a vision which reputedly made him tell his friend and secretary Br Reginald, 'Everything that I have written seems like straw to me compared to those things that I have seen and have been revealed to me',[2] he was not repudiating his monumental *Summa Theologiae*. Rather, he had surely seen that theological 'answers' are at best no more than part of a living relationship with the One from whom all life proceeds and to whom all life returns. Study and practice of faith, in communion with fellow believers, are essential to the pilgrim way that is our vocation in this world. But like the labourers in Jesus's parable, hired at different hours of the day to work in the vineyard (Matt. 20:1–16), people may be called to this way at any stage of life.

---

[2] Cf. aquinasonline.com/saint-thomas-aquinas-1224-5-1274/ (accessed 10.2.25).

An ancient saying attributed to Evagrius Ponticus (345–399) has it that the theologian is the one who prays.[3] The present meditations are anchored in prayer, in its broadest and its most specific modes, in the hope that they might offer something of value for the reader's own spiritual explorations. We are all on an adventure of knowledge of something we know to be beyond knowing. On this adventure we find that even in the face of the overwhelming mystery of pain and death there can be pointers to the eternal actuality—the loveliness, the glory, the joy and sanctity—of life.

> Let all thy days
> Till life shall end,
> Whate'er he send,
> Be filled with praise.[4]

---

[3] '153 Chapters on Prayer', chapter 60, in *The Philokalia: The Complete Text*, ed. G. E. H. Palmer and Philip Sherrard, 5 vols. (Faber & Faber, 1979–99), vol. 1, 55–71.

[4] Richard Baxter and J. H. Gurney, from the hymn 'Ye Holy Angels Bright'.

THE SPECTRE UNMASKED

There is nothing in the world more natural than death, yet equally naturally, and healthily, most of us for most of our lives prefer not to think about it. Exceptional moments—health crises, accidents, loss of one we love—break through the surface of normality, opening us to new awareness of the reality of death. Loss of a baby or child, or the premature death of a parent, sibling, or partner can leave a deep wound that the passage of time may never completely heal. But in less tragic circumstances, in the same way that a wound heals and we simply live with the scar, 'normality' returns and pushes death once again into the background. The scar may make its presence felt at times, or for one reason or another impinge on consciousness, catching us off-guard, reminding us of that different level of knowledge we carry within us, gained through loss or a brush with the essential contingency of life. But 'life must go on' and, if we allow it, the knowledge can be an invisible maturing, our more intimate acquaintanceship with mortality a source of new appreciation of life.

*

Old portraits sometimes feature a human skull, hourglass, or clock perhaps topped by a decorative grim reaper, either lurking in the shadows or placed squarely in the foreground, on a table or desk. This tradition of *memento mori*, pointing us to our mortality, paradoxically often conveys distinct relish for the subject of death. The gruesome medieval *danse macabre* of skeletons dancing with richly dressed ladies, princes and Church dignitaries, like the much more jovial Mexican Day of the Dead celebrations, has a festive energy that affirms life. Extreme sports and the allure of exploratory adventure illustrate the compelling attractiveness of 'dicing with death'. Films and games involving murder, breathtaking car chases and lethal combat make a fortune for their producers and stars. In other words, it seems death has a fascination, a horrible yet compulsive attraction for us. The feelings it arouses are complex, mixed, inadmissible, chaotic. They range from the most sublime religious, artistic and musical inspiration to the unspeakably obscene. They move and drastically disturb us. Yet in that disturbance the most profound creativity can be generated. Without death, the old adage goes, there would be no philosophy.

> We knew not that we were to live –
> Nor when we are to die –
> Our ignorance our Cuirass is –
> We wear Mortality
> As lightly as an Option Gown
> Till asked to take it off –
> By his intrusion God is known –
> It is the same with Life – [5]

*

Central to Christian faith is the traumatic, deliberately humiliating death of Jesus in the prime of his life. The humanly incomprehensible phenomenon of what we call his resurrection radically transformed how that death was seen and memorialized by those who had been close to him. Yet the trauma experienced through witnessing what one might describe as his judicial lynching, did not simply flip into unalloyed joy as awareness of his 'rising' from the dead spread among those friends. The reality of horror, fear, anger, grief, confusion, disbelief is not instantly erased by the resurrection. Despite a tendency among many Christians to celebrate the Easter mystery with a joy sanitized, so to speak, from the tormenting complexity of the heart, the Gospels speak of joy emerging out of a context of trauma-filled incredulity. The utter reversal of the natural order on 'the third day' is

---

[5] Emily Dickinson, Poem no. 1481 in *'The Poems of Emily Dickinson'* (Belknap Harvard, 2005).

wholly beyond the mind's ability to grasp. Transcending human comprehension, it inevitably inspires, at the natural level, a fear of the unknown, even within the first dawning of joy—the 'fear' that is 'the beginning of wisdom' (Prov. 9:10). This 'fear of the Lord' is not simply creaturely fear for the self, but a timeless experience of awe in which the individual is overwhelmed by a sense of the majesty and limitlessness of primal being.

Even in its collective expression, true joy is an intensely intimate experience, a liberation from controlling fears, sorrows and perhaps hitherto-unrecognized constriction and pain. The specifically Christian experience of joy is a transformative personal encounter with the risen Christ, an overwhelming gift of Pentecostal life-breathing and fire— 'Did not our hearts burn within us ... ?' (Luke 24:32)—that cannot be contained within the emoji-style world of conventional depiction. It can only be known through an affective and psychological process of reception of love, light, the Word of life, into the hell of inherited and realized suffering that lies deep in every human heart.[6] This process may be dramatically quick, or it may extend over years. It establishes the dimension of time in that of eternity. It is the essence of 'conversion', and as such is ultimately, for us all, a lifelong process.

The danger for any committed Christian is a kind of routinization of this process by emotionalism and over-familiarity. Our constant retelling of the story becomes a *de facto* foreclosure whereby we lose touch with the ever-new challenge of what has become, at the human level, merely part of our 'identity'. In consequence, well-intended

---

[6] In Eastern Orthodox tradition, which deems Christ's bodily rising from the dead to be beyond any possible figurative representation, the icon of the resurrection depicts a dynamic Christ in a mandorla of light trampling down the gates of hell, and drawing Adam and Eve up out of imprisonment. Broken locks and redundant keys are scattered over the collapsed doors. The Western tradition, powerfully expressed for instance in Piero della Francesca's fresco of the Resurrection in Sansepolcro, in Tuscany, depicts a stylized imagining of an actual moment of emergence from the tomb. Both traditions have an abstract quality that reaches deeper than conscious awareness, however profound.

Christian advice to those facing death or struggling to cope with grief can lack empathy. More than a spiritual philosophy, or recipe for moral wellness, faith is a relational knowledge permeating every dimension of our being. It is 'caught, not taught'. It must always engage with the unpredictable, anarchic, often shameful and ambivalent aspects of human reality—otherwise it is little more than a set of precepts and individual emotional conviction. The 'sure and certain hope' proclaimed in the burial service expresses something of this reality of process, in which 'hope' rather than dogmatic conviction is the one thing 'sure and certain'.[7]

> All my hope on God is founded;
> he doth still my trust renew,
> me through change and chance he guideth,
> only good and only true.
> God unknown,
> he alone
> calls my heart to be his own.[8]

---

[7] Book of Common Prayer, 'Order for the Burial of the Dead'.
[8] Robert Bridges, after Joachim Neander.

LIFE AS STORY

Every story has a beginning, middle and end. Each story is different, and can be shaped to confound conventional beginnings, middles and ends. Yet all have in common something other than merely structure: a primordial dynamic that makes a *story* rather than, say, a fact sheet, information manual, treatise, or scientific paper. Such useful forms of literature also have a beginning, middle and end, but they are not stories. A story is not ultimately 'useful'. It grips the heart, through imagination and evocation of feelings, of atmosphere, excitement, desire, pain, crisis, redemption. It takes us on a journey with twists and turns that leave us constantly asking, 'What next?' And it resolves, finally, in real time. As it ends we may be left with unanswered questions, we may be sad at saying goodbye to characters we feel have become part of our own life, we may feel let down, or we may feel a satisfying sense of completeness.

Every human life is a story, lived by the 'self' rather than narrated by an 'other'.[9] It has a beginning, middle and end. It is not merely 'useful'. It is a tale of amazement and boredom; conviction and uncertainty; illusion and disenchantment; tragedy; luck; opportunities; and often hard-to-realize blessings. The pressures and fantasies of modern life all too often encourage us to reduce this multidimensional tale to a two-dimensional, retrospective fact sheet, CV, self-promotional literature, or portfolio of fun times. But the reality of our being is at that primordial level where the heart is gripped, and we are truly engaged with the adventure of what is ahead, knowing that the structure of our story, our beginning, middle and end, is not the whole story, but part of a

---

[9] There is much philosophical discussion about the nature of the self and personal agency. The French poet Rimbaud famously declared to a friend in 1871, *Je est un autre*—'I is an other'. But making that declaration was in itself part of the poet's story.

greater wholeness of life—of which we may have intuitive glimpses throughout the narrative of our living, but which finds completeness only in the acceptance of our end.

> Yea, though I walk through the valley of the shadow of death, I will fear no evil: for thou art with me; thy rod and thy staff they comfort me. (Ps. 23:4 KJV)

Through the story of Jesus of Nazareth we are able to enter into the transcendent completeness of the universal human story. A particular character in a particular time and place, Jesus affirms the uniqueness of a human life. At the same time, by the qualities of his person, his unique history and individuality, he affirms the commonality of all human experience. In his 'human nature' he offers a relatable vision of the Divine within and beyond us all. In his Divine Nature he offers an inspiring vision for true humanity, through loving actions grounded in a knowledge beyond human explanatory power. In the completeness of his story, the human experience of completeness, beginning, middle and end, itself finds completion. Christ is 'all things and is in all' (Col. 3:11). By his arms opened wide for us on the Cross, we are taken beyond the horizon of relative, mortal consciousness. And this 'raising up' is not just something that happens at the end of the linear plot line of our life, but is the eternal 'now' of life in its fullness at any and every point of our story.

In Christ we each participate, as the unique person we are, with our particular gifts and flaws, in that all-embracing, eternal story. The role we are given, yet which we also create, adds our individuality to the infinite wholeness of being—the 'mystical Body'—that is at once wholly personal and wholly, indivisibly, unified. Every human being, however important or unimportant in others' eyes, however small and worthless they may themselves feel, contributes to the life of the kingdom of God, and enriches it, to the glory of God. In the compassion of Christ, whatever vile things we have done in our life, our sins, are finally shown up for what they are, in the light of a judgement that infinitely transcends our human capacity for assessment and punishment. 'Mercy and truth are met together; righteousness and peace have kissed each other.' (Ps. 85:10).[10] The completed story is a radically new departure, not discontinuous with the narrative of our life, but proceeding into a new idiom, the untold glory of the created cosmos and the gratuitous energy of love that made and sustains it.

> Most High, all-powerful, good Lord,
> Yours are the praises, the glory,
> and the honour and all blessing.
> To You alone, Most High, do they belong
> and no human is worthy to mention Your name.
>
> Praised be you, my Lord,
> with all Your creatures,
> especially Sir Brother Sun,
> who is the day,
> and through whom You give us light.
> And he is beautiful
> and radiant with great splendour;
> and bears a likeness of You, Most High one.
>
> Praised be You, my Lord,
> through Sister Moon and the stars,
> in heaven You formed them
> clear and precious and beautiful.
> Praised be You, my Lord,
> through Brother Wind,
> and through the air, cloudy and serene,
> and every kind of weather
> through which you give substance to your creatures.
> Praised be You, my Lord,
> through Sister water,
> who is very useful and humble
> and precious and chaste.
> Praised be You, my Lord,
> through Brother fire,
> through whom You light the night,

---

[10] Sung at Christmas, the Feast of the Incarnation.

and he is beautiful and playful
and robust and strong.

Praised be You, my Lord,
through our Sister Mother Earth,
who sustains and governs us,
and who produces various fruit
with coloured flowers and herbs.

Praised be You, my Lord,
through those who give pardon for Your love,
and bear infirmity and tribulation.
Blessed those who endure in peace,
for by You, Most High, shall they be crowned.

Praised be You, my Lord,
through our Sister Bodily Death,
from whom no one living can escape.
Woe to those who die in mortal sin.
Blessed are those whom death
will find in Your most holy will,
for the second death shall do them no harm.

Praise and bless my Lord and give Him thanks
and serve Him with great humility.[11]

---

[11] St Francis of Assisi, 'Canticle of the Creatures', translation from https://www.laudatosi.org/the-letter/the-canticle-of-creatures/ (accessed 10.2.25).

'DEATH BE NOT PROUD'[12]

In 1720 the composer Johann Sebastian Bach accompanied his employer, Prince Leopold of Anhalt-Köthen, to the Carlsbad Spa. After two months he returned home to find that his beloved wife Maria Barbara had died very suddenly, and been buried. Of their seven children, four survived into adulthood, although one died at the age of twenty-four. Bach's own parents had both died before he was ten years old. Of the thirteen children he had with his second wife Anna Magdalena, seven died in infancy. His most deeply moving music is surely informed by accumulated grief at these heartrending losses.

It is difficult for those fortunate enough to live in a society with highly developed medical technology and expertise to understand the precariousness of life without such benefits. When infant and maternal mortality are tragic exceptions to a generally happy norm of childbirth and childcare, we allow a degree of emotional investment in each child very different from that in countries where early childhood is still a highly uncertain stage of life. Similarly, our expectations as to a natural lifespan are quite different from those in less technologically developed societies, or where natural disasters, autocracies, economic exploitation and war render human life 'cheap'.

Despite these differences, the emotional and practical impacts of death in any context are fundamentally the same. Feelings are not measurable. Like physical pain they have no comparator, other than personal empathy. And where there is minimal welfare support, the practical ramifications of death become systemic and in the end equally immeasurable. Those who claim that people living in poverty and insecurity are less affected because 'it's what they're used to' demonstrate

---

[12] John Donne, 'Divine Meditation 10', in *The Complete English Poems*, ed. A. J. Smith (Penguin, 1971), This edition has excellent notes.

a callousness and disregard for human dignity entirely contrary to the teachings of every major world religion and to the fundamental concepts of human rights. It reflects a crudely quantitative view of existence, blind to the mystery of being. Yet the sheer mystery of life is the spur to all human striving, whether for knowledge and understanding, spiritual enlightenment, or monuments, material and cultural, to outlast time.

> Life is an astonishment, and it behoves us to be astonished.[13]

*

> The days of our age are threescore years and ten; and though men be so strong that they come to fourscore years, yet is their strength then but labour and sorrow; so soon passeth it away, and we are gone. (Ps. 90:10 BCP)

This proverbial scriptural definition of the natural human lifespan is not the same as a modern estimate of life expectancy. It refers only to those who survive infancy and the disasters of war and other exceptional events, whereas statistics today take an average of all lives from birth to death. Life expectancy in many parts of the world, taking in infant and maternal mortality, famine and war deaths etcetera, is well under 'threescore years and ten'. But of course many people also live longer than the overall average. Within highly developed countries meanwhile, with an average life expectancy of around, or just over, eighty, the difference between the lifespan of rich and poor is, shockingly, up to ten years.[14]

Our feelings about our own mortality are inevitably affected by general expectations across the society of which we are part. It is easy to feel, unthinkingly, that we have a right to live to at least the average age. A prognosis that we will die younger is all the harder to accept when we have such background figures to compare ourselves against.

---

[13] A widely quoted aphorism, commonly attributed to John Donne.
[14] See https://tinyurl.com/UKlife2018-20 (accessed 01.12.2024).

Battling against a potentially terminal disease or life-threatening injury, refusing to give in, is vital to survival or adaptation to a more restricted life after intensive treatment and therapy. Yet recognizing when that battle is not winnable is also vital. It is a process of deep acceptance that, rather than being defeat, is an understanding of life at a new level, an achievement of inner reconciliation with the reality of one's existence. It is a move away from self-assessment against the standards, real or imagined, of others and of the outside world, to discovery of one's own unique individual being in time, the being which only we can be.

Classical writers considered old age a curse. Much better to die in the fullness of one's strength and abilities. With modern medicine and less physically-demanding lifestyles, however, old age can be a rich and fulfilling time of life. Where it becomes problematic is when pain, frailty, dependency, mental capacity become the all-conditioning content of everyday existence. Just as there is a tipping point for younger people, where battling against a disease gives way to the exploration and active process of acceptance, so there is a tipping stage, impossible to pinpoint, when prolonging life becomes, in effect, simply a matter of extending the process of dying. The issue of assisted dying, with all its ethical, spiritual and practical complexities, is one that medical advances has made impossible to ignore.

The old, relatively simple notion of a natural human lifespan no longer holds. What constitutes 'natural' in a world in which physical existence is sustained only by surgical, pharmacological and technological interventions unknown to most of human history, and still today available only to a certain proportion of the world's population? The decision to switch off a life-support machine or, in the absence of any effective cure or palliation, to end a torturous physical existence, can only be taken in a spirit of loving care that speaks of the humility and compassion of Christ.

Meanwhile, in dogmatically asserting the sanctity of life it is important to have a holistic view. Our existence as individuals cannot be divorced from the socio-political context to which we individually contribute and by which we are shaped. There is a certain dishonesty in proclaiming the absolute value of individual human life while failing to take equally seriously social inequalities that directly shorten many lives. As already mentioned, within a highly affluent country such as the UK the poor have a life expectancy up to ten years less than the rich. This problem has solutions, if only we had the political will to apply them. If we truly believed in the sanctity of every life we would recognize that reducing the life-limiting conditions of poverty within our society is as intensely spiritual an issue as that of assisted dying.

The same applies even more starkly at the global level. The richest countries of the world, including the UK, benefit from systemic global inequities that lead to poor countries being unable to fund crucial educational and health infrastructure. Millions of lives are affected. Yet the wealthiest nations, including the UK, seek to block moves to mitigate these inequalities. For instance, at the time of writing, while the vast majority of countries at the UN support legislation that would end tax evasion by multinational companies, thus enabling poor countries to invest in essential infrastructure, the wealthy countries, where most multinationals are based, have actively opposed it.[15] Their opposition perpetuates chronic poverty and early death throughout the world. Politically-motivated military alliances, in which the lives of men, women and children are secondary to our national self-interest and putative values, are of course equally part of the debate. People living in affluent democracies have, through parliamentary process, the power to address such issues.

Sins of omission are as grave as sins of commission. Insofar as we fail to see assisted dying within this wider perspective of the curtailing of life we are, spiritually speaking, applying double standards. I would argue also that the hugely important issue of abortion should similarly take into account the 'privatizing' of sanctity of life, such that collective social issues are not recognized as

---

[15] See https://tinyurl.com/7283-0366-9-20 (accessed 01.12.2024).

essentially spiritual. However, meaningful discussion of this is beyond the scope of the present essay.

> I know that my redeemer liveth, and that he shall stand at the latter day upon the earth: And though after my skin worms destroy this body, yet in my flesh shall I see God: Whom I shall see for myself, and mine eyes shall behold, and not another.   (Job 19:25–7 KJV)

BODY AND SOUL

A soul suspended between a longing to be free of this life yet at the same time fear of dying, is a soul in torment. But what is the soul? Is there such a thing? What is its relationship to the body? Is it part of human 'nature' and therefore part of how we define 'natural'? Or is it of God, the 'Divine Spark', thus supernatural?

We could perhaps at least say it is that which most essentially defines our human, as opposed to animal, identity. That is not to deny our animal nature, but it is a claim that we are not defined by that alone. Equally it is not to deny that animals have their own distinct soul, which shares a degree of kinship with ours, and which we cannot abuse without diminishing our humanity. Many traditional cultures around the world indeed see their physical environment—mountains, springs, rivers, lakes, rocks, forests—as endowed with a sacred identity. Given the deadening environmental abuse wreaked by global materialist consumerism, we urgently need to recognize the spiritual implications of destroying nature, and to recover a sense of our obligations toward the life of the supposedly inanimate world, charged as it is with the creative stamp of the Divine.

Some Christians regrettably distrust such veneration of nature as 'new paganism', as if by celebrating the love and awesome mystery and purpose of God manifest in the wonders of creation we are somehow worshiping nature rather than the Creator. This distrust, fencing off the human soul from its creaturely context, reflects an insecure faith. By confessing, in the broadest sense, our creatureliness through relationship with the rest of creation, while honouring the responsibilities we have toward the rest of creation by virtue of our human soul, we joyfully proclaim that in Christ, and our participation in the Body of Christ, ultimately the whole created order is redeemed.

Atheists of course dismiss the need for any concept of a soul. Yet secular ideas of human dignity, respect for life, universal rights must be grounded in some ultimate denominator of value. What might that be? There is no universal agreement. *Pace* the American Declaration of Independence, history shows all too clearly that innate equality, for instance, is *not* 'self-evident'.[16] For a Christian, what makes all human beings equal in dignity and worth is the seal of the image of God. This is the fundamental mould of our humanity. Formed from the dust of the ground, we have life 'breathed' into us by God.[17] Inanimate clay is transformed by the exhalation of creative Spirit into it. After his resurrection Jesus 'breathed' the Holy Spirit upon his disciples (John 20:22). Spirit and soul—*pneuma* (literally, breath) and *psyche*—are different aspects of our person, but such words are insufficient to capture the reality of what they signify, and their use in the New Testament is not entirely consistent. Bearing in mind the broad connotations of 'soul' in English, as in putting 'heart and soul' into something, we might define soul as that indefinable energy and unique personal quality that determines our identity at its deepest level. Theologically it is the Divine Breath of the loving Creator that animates our being and bestows upon us both blessings and responsibilities. Essential to our bodily existence, distinct from our body yet conditioned by our mortal actions, it is destined to stand before God for judgement on the last 'day'.

> One soul in the immensity of its intelligence is greater and more excellent than the whole world. The Ocean is but the drop of a bucket to it, the Heavens but a centre, the Sun obscurity, and all Ages but as one day. It being by its understanding a Temple of Eternity, and God's omnipresence, between which and the whole world there is no proportion.[18]

Belief in the existence of a soul characterized by some kind of immortality has a long history and remains widespread, though not

---

[16] Cf. The American Declaration of Independence: 'We hold these truths to be self-evident, that all men are created equal … '.
[17] Cf. the two accounts in Genesis, 1:27 and 2:7.
[18] Thomas Traherne, *Centuries of Meditations* (Mowbray, 1960), II.70.

universal. Different understandings and definitions reflect a vast range of human experience and speculation, from ghosts interacting, usually unhappily, with the temporal world, to transmigration through cycles of karma, to spiritual enjoyment of an eternal paradise. In the time of Jesus, the priestly Sadducees denied the existence of an afterlife, while the Pharisees, with an oral tradition (later written down, to form the Talmud) supplementing the Torah, believed in resurrection of the righteous. Christian tradition proclaims resurrection of our whole person, soul and body:

> If the Spirit of him who raised Jesus from the dead dwells in you, he who raised Christ from the dead will give life to your mortal bodies also through his Spirit who dwells in you. (Rom. 8:11)[19]

What form our resurrected body will take is addressed by St Paul in his first Letter to the early Church in Corinth:

> But someone will ask, "How are the dead raised? With what kind of body do they come?" Fool! What you sow does not come to life unless it dies. And as for what you sow, you do not sow the body that is to be but a bare seed, perhaps of wheat or of some other grain. But God gives it a body as he has chosen and to each kind of seed its own body. ... What is sown is perishable; what is raised is imperishable. It is sown in dishonour; it is raised in glory. It is sown in weakness, it is raised in power. It is sown a physical body; it is raised a spiritual body.
> (1 Cor. 15.35–49)

The resurrection body thus has a form that can in no way be conceptualized from the 'bare seed' that is sown. Although organically originating in the seed, there is a radical disjunction between what is sown and what is raised. By contrast, when it comes to the soul we have a sense of continuity across the divide of death. We know that when we die our perishable body will need to be disposed of, and in practical terms, planning funeral arrangements with family and others in advance can be part of the process of addressing anxieties aroused

---

[19] Cf. also the Apostles' Creed: 'I believe in ... the resurrection of the body, and life everlasting.'

by the approaching end of life. Choosing funeral readings, music, symbolic actions and so forth can help articulate and relieve unspoken questions and feelings. Within such practical discussions is the broader question, usually implicit rather than explicit, of the relationship between body and soul. What is the significance of the physical body, that it merits such ceremony? How do we best honour the person who has left us, not merely in the recitation of their achievements and qualities, but in how we continue to relate to them after they are gone?

It is common, especially in the weeks after bereavement, for those grieving to continue to speak to the person who has died as if they were still present. They may also 'see' that beloved person, performing some familiar task perhaps, or 'visiting' with words of reassurance. Such *post mortem* experiences tend to become less vivid with time, though certain memories may always retain a powerful sensory aspect. It is natural to seek to preserve a relationship beyond death through physical tokens of the departed—tending graves, wearing the other's jewellery, treasuring photos—but when this develops into emotional clinging, the bereaved can become blocked from their own continued living. Tokens of the departed, and at a collective level statues and monuments, acquire a kind of talismanic status. For some, spiritualism is felt to be a way of maintaining relationship with those in 'the undiscovered country from whose bourn no traveller returns'.[20] Rather than condemning out of hand those who seek such comfort, we should as Christians recognize that individuals' sensibility and experience of the 'spirit world' are as varied as aesthetic and other sensory faculties. What matters is how we interpret counter-rational experiences, and how far we allow ourselves to become psychologically dependent on them.

It is surely through the quality of our living that we best honour the departed ('If only my Mum/Dad could see me now … '), in the memories we choose to dwell on, and in the integrity with which we look back and consider the virtues and vices of those who have died. In offering prayers for them we continue to hold them in our earthly

---

[20] *Hamlet*, Act 3, scene i.

care by commending them to the eternal care of the maker and sustainer of all. We may not necessarily subscribe to a fully-worked-out doctrine of purgatory, but we present before God our love for those we remember, who in some sense still shape who we are, and with whom we share equally in an eternal present of time and timelessness:

> I am convinced that neither death, nor life, nor angels, nor rulers, nor things present, nor things to come, nor powers, nor height, nor depth, nor anything else in all creation, will be able to separate us from the love of God in Christ Jesus our Lord. (Rom. 8:38–9)

It is that love, always anticipating ours, that stirs and empowers life, in a redemptive dynamic that unifies every dimension of the created order.

It may be that our relationship with the person who died was difficult, or worse. Perhaps we are left with internal tensions, feelings of resentment and negativity, residue of unresolved conflict. The ancient caution against speaking ill of the dead may need to be overridden in the name of justice. Such emotions can greatly complicate the grieving process, and it may be that professional counselling can help. Anger at God, or at life in general, is a very natural though often unacknowledged reaction to bereavement. In close relationships we can even feel irrational anger towards the dying or departed: how dare they abandon us? Feelings of guilt at such (often unavowed) anger add yet another level of complexity to grief. Suicide, for all its tragedy, can also precipitate intense anger against the person who for whatever reason has taken their own life. Where deliberate violence or irresponsible behaviour was the cause of death, anger and bitterness can become all-consuming. The issue of forgiveness is raised below.

In the end we and the departed, and any third parties, alike remain accountable to God, the final arbiter, who will, if approached with no holding back, receive all our anger, all our pain, and grant us, in time, the ability to move on without needing constantly to refer to the past.

*

One of the classic subjects of Western religious art is the *Pietà*, depicting Mary, the mother of Jesus, cradling the dead body of her son across her lap—mirroring that other great religious motif, the Madonna and Child. In a *Pietà* Christ's body, taken down from the Cross, continues somehow in its very lifelessness to be charged with life. Likewise, in the period between a person's death and their burial or cremation, the body usually continues to be referred to as 'he' or 'she'. Although objectively a corpse, to anyone with any personal connection it cannot be merely an 'it'. We seek in all sorts of ways to connect the physical remains with the person, body and soul, we knew.

Personhood is inescapably bodily, because we are what has been termed 'ensouled matter'.[21] So a body might be embalmed, dressed in best suit and tie, or other meaningful clothing, accompanied by jewellery, a cross, a bottle of whisky … whatever might symbolize a once live relationship. The style of coffin and flowers, cloths, photos placed on it, all speak of a personal reality once completely dependent on the body that has now to be disposed of.

The sheer physicality of grief cannot be overstated. The loss, loneliness, oppressive emptiness of living room and bed, are experienced viscerally. Headstones, plaques, rose bushes, trees, benches … the memories stored in heart and mind find expression in physical things which, like an infant's transitional object, are a kind of companion towards a new reality. They communicate the personal to those who never knew the person, providing a counterweight of objectivity for an otherwise potentially destabilizing subjectivity. They create, as it were, a sacred thread, connecting the dead, the mourner and the stranger. This can be felt over centuries, as we see from the pyramids, neolithic burial chambers and other such funerary sites. Like all physical existence, however, memorials are vulnerable—to erosion, vandalism, depredation. As the person who has passed ceases to be a presence in the lives of all but those who were closest to them, there

---

[21] Cf. Matthew S. Vest, *Embodied Soul and Ensouled Body*, in *Treating the Body in Medicine and Religion: Jewish, Christian, and Islamic Perspectives*, ed. John J. Fitzgerald and Ashley John Moyse (Routledge, 2021).

is an inevitable process of forgetfulness. 'I had not thought death had undone so many.'[22] Personal experience is absorbed into the flow of time, the anonymity of normality, the discipline and ritual of remembrance. Bones and ashes, however, continue to have spiritual significance. Tomb robberies, plunder of battlefield corpses, desecration of graves remind us of humanity's capacity for cynicism and inhumanity. Yet we find such actions cynical and inhuman precisely because overwhelmingly there persists a sense of the connectedness between human bodily remains and the sacred reality of personhood.

---

[22] T. S. Eliot, *The Wasteland*.

THE SANCTITY OF THE BODY

> As doth the pith, which, lest our bodies slack,
> Strings fast the little bones of neck, and back;
> So by the soul doth death string heaven and earth;
> For when our soul enjoys this her third birth,
> (Creation gave her one, a second, grace,)
> Heaven is as near, and present to her face,
> As colours are, and objects, in a room
> Where darkness was before, when tapers come.[23]

The connection of body and soul, however we might understand 'soul', is nowadays perhaps most commonly addressed in terms of the difference between brain and mind, and the so-called 'hard problem' of consciousness. Research into the influence of the gut biome on our brain, however, suggests that the brain needs to be seen holistically as part of our body, rather than as the effectively autonomous, all-controlling determinant of 'mind' and of who we are.

Integral to a holistic understanding of who we are, are the crude physical processes of birth and death, and 'enjoyment'. In Donne's lines the anatomical imagery is essential to the spiritual message. In speaking of a second birth, by grace, he alludes to the Gospel requirement that we must lose our life to find it. 'Whoever gains his soul will lose it, and whoever loses his soul for my sake will gain it.' (Matt. 10:39) 'No-one can see the kingdom of God without being born from above.' (John 3:3). He strikingly presents physical death as the connection between earth and heaven, with the soul facilitating the connection, and making of death an enjoyed 'third birth', into a world of colour, recognizable forms and light, as opposed to previous

---

[23] John Donne, 'Of the Progress of the Soul: The Second Anniversary', from the *Funeral Elegies*.

(earthly) darkness. The 'pith' that holds the vertebrae together is our spinal cord, the major channel of our central nervous system. The anatomy may not be strictly correct, but it conveys powerfully a materiality of the soul that is more than 'mind'.

The soul's second birth, its dying to the ego-self and being 'born again', changes a person. Outwardly there may not be visible change, but the direction of that person's life will be altered. Inner change will, in due course, manifest in outward consequences. This redirection of life, which can come about with dramatic suddenness or as a gradual 'labour' of realization, foreshadows the soul's 'third birth' into heaven. And the means by which the soul can enjoy its third birth is the body, the seed 'sown in dishonour' and 'raised in glory', 'sown in weakness' and 'raised in power' (1 Cor. 15:43).

In the 'dishonour' of physical debility, extreme illness, or disastrous bodily impairment, disgust at the body is entirely understandable. Suicidal feelings are common, perhaps almost inevitable. In situations of anguish of soul, mental distress, emotional abandonment, the body's innate survival instinct can turn against itself in life-endangering self-harm and suicide. Working through despair, self-hate, self-disgust, is a heroic struggle, in which the key transformative factors are unconditional love and affirmation of the dignity of the body, whatever its condition.

*

When evidence of a massacre comes to light we are horrified and outraged. Mass graves testify to a reduction of humanity to soulless, purely quantifiable matter. Such desecration of 'ensouled matter' exposes the inner dehumanization of the perpetrators. We are horrified not simply on utilitarian grounds of fear for ourselves if such behaviour were to be left unchecked by moral sanctions, but because we sense that such brutality reflects a disfiguring capacity for self-desecration within our species. It is violation of the Divine Image that is the essential matrix of our humanity.

Use of starvation as a weapon of war, terrorist random murder and the de facto indiscriminate slaughter of civilian populations likewise reflect a desacralized mind, a self-justifying logic that is in fact blood sacrifice to a false god—nationalist or ethnic identity, utopian ideal, graven image of religious absolutism.

Those whose job or circumstances bring them in contact with the human body in its most shockingly injured, torn and decomposing states suffer trauma that is not always sufficiently recognized. Images and memories of the stench of decaying flesh cause nightmares not only for those who have been on the frontline of wars, but also for police, emergency service workers and undertakers' staff. Train and bus drivers who have been unable to avoid killing people who have jumped in front of their vehicles are affected for life. Content moderators for the major global technology platforms are paid abusively low wages and receive wholly inadequate mental support to deal with the extreme pornography and often real-time violence that comes at them from the screen. To some extent people in such jobs become inured to what they see, and black humour is a temporary escape valve. But there is a fine line between professional detachment and depersonalizing, ultimately dehumanizing indifference. When personal survival is at stake, by all accounts the sight of dead bodies can become normalized, the initial shock being perhaps absorbed into self-protective objectivization. But when any human being is accounted a physically embodied abstraction rather than an individual soul, the door has been opened to the worst of evils. The only way back, the only *salvation*, is through acts of self-giving compassion, whereby the reality of the individual soul is once again revealed in its life-determining, transcendent materiality.

Soul is the relational core of who we are, interacting with other souls through the physical body it animates. When someone dies, or is presumed dead, and family and friends have no physical body to mourn over and lay to rest, a gaping void is felt. Relatives of 'the disappeared' living under dictatorships around the world clamour to know the location of the bodies of their loved ones, risking their own lives in doing so. Whether through repatriation of the body of someone who has died abroad, the witness of war cemeteries as in the north of France and Belgium, or a murderer's final confession of where their victim's body is buried, reconnection with physical remains helps bring emotional closure. The vital connectedness of soul and body, and its interconnectedness with other ensouled bodies through love, represents the invisible 'pith' uniting earthly reality in all its uncertainty and often ugly, tragic cruelty, with that other reality that is joy, unbounded meaningfulness and ineradicable beauty.

Johann Sebastian Bach reportedly said that anyone could write as good music as he if they worked hard. Of course he had a unique gift. But he clearly also had a phenomenal capacity for hard work and exceptional gusto for life. By the sheer physicality of breath through wood and metal, plucking of wire, horsehair drawn across gut, sticks beating on hide and exercise of human vocal cords, he expressed 'ensouled matter' at a consummate level. We all have unique gifts. And each of us, in our own way, with our particular gifts, is called to work and enjoy, to love, to face our griefs and disasters with courage, in a spirit of compassion and self-dedication, to share with others in our common human condition a 'music' that will harmonize, console and uplift. This music is bodily as well as spiritual, because our physical body is 'a temple of the Holy Spirit within you' (1 Cor. 6:19). The supreme music is, for a Christian, the Logos of God, the Christ who became incarnate, was killed, descended into hell[24] and is raised to the heights, and through whom we, participating in Christ's Body by our way of living in the flesh, are raised through death to an infinitely and eternally greater sphere of existence.

> The snares of death encompassed me;
> the pains of hell took hold of me;
> by grief and sorrow was I held.
> Then I called upon the name of the Lord:
> 'O Lord, I beg you, deliver my soul.'
> Gracious is the Lord and righteous;

---

[24] Cf. the Apostles' Creed and 1 Peter 3:18–22.

our God is full of compassion.
The Lord watches over the simple;
I was brought very low and he saved me.
Turn again to your rest, O my soul,
for the Lord has been gracious to you.
For you have delivered my soul from death,
my eyes from tears and my feet from falling.
I will walk before the Lord
in the land of the living.

        (Ps. 116:3–9 Common Worship Psalter)

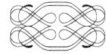

CONFRONTING REALITY WITH COURAGE

Courage is not fearlessness. Courage is the way we face reality despite deep and often disabling fear. Fearlessness is a wonderful quality, which can inspire and motivate others. However, it can also be reckless and endanger the lives of others. Courage takes account of others in a way that fearlessness cannot, because fearlessness is not alive to danger, even though it might be energized by it. Yet the two are not absolutely distinct: fearless acts of courage are performed by people who often, after the event, dismiss their heroism with phrases like, 'It just felt the right thing to do.' The distinction is only important when ordinary unheroic people become worried that they are failing in courage.

It is entirely natural to fear death, 'the great unknown'. Not to be fearful at the prospect of one's own extinction would suggest a certain indifference to life. Having said that, everyone's circumstances are different. Extreme suffering and loss of the capacity to 'live' in any meaningful way, beyond merely extending physical existence, can lead to a positive desire for death. And when this life is viewed as essentially illusory or merely part of a greater cycle of being, as in certain spiritual traditions, death is, in a sense, just as illusory or relative as life. Dogmatic materialists find comfort (they might dispute the word) in the language of atoms and randomness, and paradoxically such language can sometimes resemble that of mystical religion. When personal life is seen as secondary to some social value such as honour, or to an ideology or political or religious cause, death can be welcomed as a means to a higher end. Even in these cases, however, it is probably rare for people genuinely to experience no fear. And for most of us, however philosophically prepared we might believe ourselves to be, there is surely still some element of trepidation, not to mention the animal instinct of the body to survive, when the end is in sight.

Courage, therefore, is our engagement with fear, our willingness to accept the fact of our mortality and work toward a state in which we are at peace with that fact. Traditionally referred to as fortitude, it is one of the historic Cardinal Virtues described by Plato, discussed by Aristotle and adopted by the early Church as foundational human virtues.[25] 'I've often wondered what it will be like to die,' I remember someone saying to me. 'Now I'm finding out.'

*

Few of us are really able to come to terms with death on our own, although in situations where people die alone, with no-one to support them, we can hope and pray that they are granted an inner grace of at least a degree of acceptance, so that they are able to meet death with some mitigation of the torment of solitariness, anger and despair. Most of us in normal life situations, however, depend on support and encouragement—that is, instilling of courage—from others. It is not a weakness to need such encouragement. Accepting our dependence on others is itself an act of courage that strengthens us to go further in the journey of self-discovery that, amazingly, can be a gift of the last stage of life.

The Latin word *cor*, meaning heart, is the root of courage. Facing reality is not a state of mind, but of the heart, and the heart expresses itself in an infinite variety of ways that cannot be reduced to rational or theoretical prescripts. *Le cœur a ses raisons que la raison ne connaît point* (loosely translated, 'the heart has its own reasoning, of which reason has no conception').[26] This axiom, derived from the seventeenth-century thinker Blaise Pascal, is generally nowadays applied to romantic love. However, Pascal was writing about knowledge of God,

---

[25] Prudence, justice, fortitude, and temperance. Christian writers added to these the three so-called Theological Virtues—faith, hope, and love (Latin *caritas*)—identified by St Paul in 1 Cor. 13 and elsewhere.
[26] Cf. Blaise Pascal, *Pensées* (E. P. Dutton & Co., Inc., 1958), 'Article XXIV:5'. This edition has a helpful introduction by T. S. Eliot.

asserting that it is through the heart, not the intellect, that we come to know, or at least have some apprehension of, God. For Christians that knowledge is mediated essentially through the physicality of nature and of the incarnate Christ.

The heart expresses itself often in modest bodily gestures—a glance, a kiss, the stroke of a hand, or, in hospital for instance, help in taking a sip of water, provision of clean pyjamas, adjustment of the angle of the bed. The subtlety of the heart's language is much abused in a society where 'make love' is often no more than a euphemism for genital sex. In fact perhaps the most profound expression of love, of the deepest intelligence of the heart, is simple physical presence.

In times of grief, or in the final weeks and days of someone's life, simply to sit without necessarily even talking, allowing that person to speak if they wish to, listening, not imposing any desire to be helpful or wise, can be the most generous, comforting, life-affirming thing to do. In that seemingly inactive act, unconditionally spending time with that person, we express solidarity. A readiness to respond to little requests—in hospital, look for a nurse, go to the hospital shop, pass on a message, or at home, clean up, help bathe and shave—speaks physically the language of the heart. When offered gladly, sharing some of our own life's time with another human being as they approach the end of their time is a sacrificial gift that can bring remarkable joy.

In other instances it may be talk that is needed, rather than silence. Whatever state of health we are in, the continuance of normal life, reminders of the beauty and comedy of life, gossip, a haircut, a political discussion, can take us out of ourselves and keep us connected with the world out there. Diagnosis of a terminal condition and serious bereavement are almost always a shock, sometimes devastating, overturning plans for the future, bringing unanticipated disruptions to everyday life, and creating emotional turmoil. To maintain an equilibrium, to see things in focus, can be a struggle. Life becomes a blur, with so much to be thought through and sorted, between medical appointments, ongoing and worsening symptoms and side-effects of treatment. As life becomes more confined by a terminal condition, or as grief is painfully worked through, or tortoise-pace recovery from catastrophic injury or aggressive treatment proceeds, having friends who can be relied on and who visit without leaving us exhausted by their visit, is an enormous blessing.

*

'You find out who your real friends are,' is a common experience of those coping with drastic health and emotional problems. It is easy to be disappointed, even embittered, by the failure of long-term friends or family members to 'be there' when most needed. But we need to recognize that people react in all sorts of different ways when a relative or friend becomes seriously ill or hospitalized. Some friends were 'funtime' friends. Their inability to cope with relationships when the fun has run out is their problem. It is saddening, but does not invalidate good memories from the past. Others are temperamentally unable to face visiting. It is as if the sight of illness or injury terrifies them, perhaps arousing some hidden phobia, or stirring a deeply suppressed memory. Others find they are too busy for anything but a dash in with a card and flowers. We feel perhaps they might have stayed longer ... but it is all too easy to forget, even after just a day or so of confinement, how frenetic and stressful normal life can be, and how one's own indisposition or hospitalization is adding to that stress. Yet others might visit and want to be sympathetic and encouraging, but feel awkward at having no obvious useful task to perform, and worried about what to say and not say, especially if recovery is uncertain. There are then those visitors who see us as a captive audience, to be regaled with *their* surgical history and anecdotes of medical dramas, and who fail to notice their audience is smiling through gritted teeth or has fallen asleep.

Within the maelstrom of thoughts and feelings commonly experienced when undergoing a course of uncertain life-saving treatment, or when informed that treatment has not been successful, the patient is sometimes also burdened by having to cheer up visitors who are not coping well with their own emotions. This can be more than a little wearisome. On top of the emotional and psychological struggle of coming to terms with our condition, the physical discomfort, pain and exhaustion, and the tangled practicalities of financial and legal demands, we can find ourselves additionally having to comfort a friend or relative who has come to tell us how overwhelmed they are by our being so unwell. In extreme cases we are effectively being accused of selfishness by allowing ourselves to become ill.

Although it is difficult to be sympathetic toward such self-centredness, it is perhaps a reminder of how fragile our rational 'civilized' identities are. The stock image of death is a skeleton with a scythe, but another, with a different emphasis, might be a plough, turning the earth, our bodily element—

> In the sweat of thy face shalt thou eat bread, till thou return unto the ground; for out of it wast thou taken: for dust thou *art*, and unto dust shalt thou return. (Gen. 3.19 KJV)

For some people, even the suggestion of death can trigger irrational anxieties and griefs, guilt reactions, anger, and aggressive compensatory behaviour. Every situation and relationship is unique, but where the familiar terrain of a relationship is suddenly ploughed up, the relationship may become volatile. Long-buried memories can be reawakened. Regrets, recriminations, self-recrimination, disappointed hopes can manifest in twisted feelings that cause pain to all. Uncertainty about the future will make such reactions all the more volatile.

By contrast, where there is a positive relationship, that volatility will settle, and a new stage of relationship develop—fresh shoots in the turned land. Where treatment leads to recovery, the bond with friends and loved ones can be found to have become all the stronger. Where the condition proves terminal, those weeks and days can, despite all the difficulties and sadness, be a hugely precious time of recollection and togetherness. Courageous recognition of how things stand cannot alter the facts of the situation, but it can establish a stage of life, however short, when a new intensity of relationship can be experienced, hurts and misunderstandings from the past be healed, and moments of intimacy be enjoyed, that will be treasured memories in the future. Other relationships, perhaps with someone who had never seemed particularly close before, or for instance with hospice staff and volunteers, can also be formed, bringing new understandings and perspectives on the 'astonishment' of life.

The process of grieving for a loved one often starts before their death, and can to some extent, in a process of mutual encouragement, be shared between both the person dying and the person who will have to adjust to life without them. This sharing may be of the most down-to earth kind: before her death at a cruelly young age, a devout Christian friend of mine with three dependent children told her husband that he should re-marry as soon as possible. It proved a happy directive.

Even when all has been well talked through and prepared, however, the impact of grief is not wholly predictable. Nor can the process of working through grief be hurried. Almost certainly there will be feelings of dreadful isolation as life moves on for everyone else, and the bereaved person is left struggling to manage the void in their life. This feeling of isolation can be made worse by a sense of peer pressure to 'get over it'. Some withdraw into themselves, not wishing to be 'the ghost at the feast' in social gatherings. And while for some, bereavement can in fact be liberation from an oppressive or abusive relationship ('I hear her hair has turned quite gold from grief,' Algernon remarks of Lady Hanbury in Oscar Wilde's *The Importance of Being Earnest*), for many it may feel as if 'part of me has died', and they are also therefore in a sense having to mourn and dispose of something within themselves that is no longer alive. In some cultures people adopt a visible sign, perhaps black clothing or a black armband, to show they are in mourning, and although this in turn can become oppressive, it may also be helpful at a certain stage. In the absence of such conventions, most people try to put on a brave face, but that is not endlessly sustainable. Anti-depressants are a modern response to grief in wealthy societies. In some cases these can undoubtedly be helpful. Often, however, they seem a rather too easy resort for what is not in itself a clinical problem. In the end there is no painless or quick solution to grief. As generation upon generation has known, it is up to us to face reality with courage—and to discover through doing so that it is not in our strength alone, in exercise of the cardinal virtues, however admirable, that we truly *live*. Courage opens the way to a different level of being. Our 'real friends' are those who out of love are willing to accompany us through the dark times, and to share in the moments of reminiscence, laughter and hope for the future that are a source of inner blessedness.

> No-one has greater love than this, to lay down one's life for one's friends. You are my friends if you do what I command you.
> (John 15:13–14)

*

Beginning with a reflection on the nature of courage and our need for mutual encouragement in times of crisis, this chapter has explored some of the ways that courage is shown in often humble practical actions and attitudes. More often than not, courage is unapparent, deceptively unheroic. In most cases it is perseverance in the face of endless petty, demoralizing, painful and humiliating challenges, in a spirit of deep appreciation of being, despite all that has to be endured. It is an existential decision of the will to be true to what is wondrous in this unaccountable adventure we call life.

But courage does not only face toward individual problems. Nowadays more than ever, courage is required to face societal issues, as the scale of mass death and potential global annihilation confronts old assumptions and traditional religious teaching with almost unanswerable challenges. In 1952, as Christians wrestled with their faith in the light of the huge questions raised by the atrocities of the Holocaust and the nuclear anxieties of the early Cold War, the German philosopher and theologian Paul Tillich published a seminal book *The Courage to Be*.[27] In its analysis and proposals the book remains as relevant as ever. Tillich sees God as the ground of being, and the answer to anxiety about death, about non-being, lies in our simple acceptance of *being*. It does not require conscious assent to any religious dogma or practice of faith, but locates the Divine in the heart of human experience, the simple *courage* to be what we are, in the face of a world in which, for so many, religious certainties offer nothing meaningful.

In Jesus, I believe, we see the supreme exemplar of this courage — the courage to be wholly the human person he was, and wholly *being* itself, transcendent in humility. In the Body of Christ the individual person and the corporate body of the Church are intimately and incomprehensibly one. While we have witnessed — and some still mourn — the death of the old idea of Christendom, new and contested forms of Christian identity have emerged. New forms of evangelistic zeal place greater stress on individual faith. New approaches in theology, science, and sociology have impacted on the traditional vocabulary of Christian practice. Even more than in the past, individual believers have now to contend not only with secularist movements, atheism, and other faiths, but also rival orthodoxies and types of spirituality amongst Christians. This makes all the harder discussion of traditional religious beliefs about the after-life, salvation, and judgement in the context of terminal care.

Those with a strong belief, who see in Jesus humanity's redeemer from the fear-dependent tyranny of evil and death, naturally long to share their belief with others who are sceptical or disbelieving, especially those to whom they are close. They feel that as a non-believer approaches the end of their life, if only they would open their heart to Jesus they would find salvation. Unfortunately in practice this sometimes amounts to the believer effectively wanting the non-believer to replicate what they themselves have experienced, rather than helping them discover their own relationship with Jesus the Anointed One, or the Holy Spirit or the transcendent Father. The

---

[27] Paul Tillich, *The Courage to Be* (Yale University Press, 1954).

courage of faith required of the believer here is to let go their sense of what faith *should* look like, and allow the Spirit truly to lead.

In the past, it was considered vital to try to secure the deathbed conversion of a sceptic or atheist, even if their profession of faith was out of terror of hellfire rather than embrace of Gospel values. Nowadays, with more honest recognition of the drastic historical failings and abuses of institutional religion, such 'conversion tactics' are probably less common. Many people would view it as quite inappropriate, a form of bullying, to try in a cerebral, credal sense to 'convert' someone in their final days and hours. However much we may long for a non-believer to share our faith, even perhaps believing that non-belief destines that person to damnation, our task is surely: first to remember that we ourselves are sinners, and thus the way we understand our own faith is potentially subject to the distorting effects of sin; to respect the God-given dignity and vulnerability of the person for whom we are concerned; to plead for them in our private prayers; to ask for the intercession of the saints on their behalf; and most importantly, to mediate the loving, life-bestowing presence of Christ through basic kindness, unpressurizing statement of our beliefs but otherwise careful withholding of personal opinions and desires, and simple willingness to be alongside them in the long silences of their final journey. God alone is judge and will know the inner state of that person's soul.

Many people approaching the end of their life, or preparing for an operation they know they may not survive, do, however, wish to talk about faith and belief. It takes a different kind of courage to accompany these 'explorers' into the deepest areas of the heart and psyche—particularly when, as in England, cultural norms militate against serious discussion of spiritual matters, and we are not used to talking about serious things without flippancy or irony. It is surprising how many practising Christians, even after years of churchgoing, lack confidence in praying and speaking of their faith. The act of courage required in such situations is to speak simply and sincerely about what their faith means to them; to not worry about lack of fluency or theological terminology; and to know that the only 'expertise' when it comes to spiritual matters is humility, genuine love and compassion, and practical companionship. *Cor ad cor loquitur*: heart speaks to heart.

Part of 'practical companionship' may then be to help bridge the gap that so often exists between non-churchgoers and church professionals. While a cold-call visit by a priest or minister may be counter-productive, a trusted broker could perhaps help effect a transformative encounter. By the grace of Christ, in the companionship (literally, bread-sharing) of open discussion, it is possible sometimes, even in the midst of pain and medicated consciousness, and despite continuing hesitancy and doubt, to come to that place of naked honesty, meaningful unknowing, where Christian prayer and sacrament can bring a new level of peace and joy of heart.

> Give me my scallop shell of quiet,
> My staff of faith to walk upon,
> My scrip of joy, immortal diet,
> My bottle of salvation,
> My gown of glory, hope's true gage,
> And thus I'll take my pilgrimage.[28]

---

[28] Sir Walter Raleigh, from 'The Passionate Man's Pilgrimage', written shortly before his execution.

FAITH AND PRAYER IN A TERMINAL CONTEXT

Only God knows who truly has faith. 'Many who are first will be last, and the last will be first.' (Matt. 19:30). Those with a self-aware religious faith will at least have a framework of prayer and practice to help support them in situations of health crisis and grief. But religious faith is not a pill that magically does away with natural human experiences of trepidation, worry, confusion, fear and roller-coaster emotions. It is not uncommon for people of faith to find their faith severely tested, and indeed lacking, at such momentous times. This can add to the confusion and anxiety precipitated by receiving 'bad news'.

At the other end of the belief spectrum, those with a strong conviction that human existence is nothing more than an ever-changing arrangement of atoms and reconfigurations of energy, may be content to rest in the psychological security of that belief. Many, however, are somewhere in between, more agnostic than atheist, uncomfortable with the absoluteness of conviction, whether theist or atheist, and possibly viewing the mindset of conviction itself with scepticism. For such individuals, and for those whose conviction may have been shaken by the reality of their approaching end or devastating loss, there is little obvious comfort or security. 'Bad news' can trigger disturbing spiritual upheaval on top of the other natural human responses. They will have simply to face whatever comes with courage.

Some may experience a desire to 'pray', yet feel that since they have no religious belief, it would be meaningless or hypocritical to succumb to that desire. However, while the deep feelings of every individual should be respected in all their complexity, it may be that the problem is more one of conventional mental associations around words like 'belief', 'prayer' and 'God' than of the reality to which those words point. The language of conviction, of conventional religious faith or philosophical integrity, can lead to a self-consciousness that inhibits understanding of faith at its simplest, essential level.

'I believe; help my unbelief!' (Mark 9:24)[29]

The 'superstitious' desire to pray should not be despised, or self-censored due to a lack of belief. Prayer is not dependent on conscious assent to the existence of God. To draw an analogy, we do not have to understand solar energy to enjoy its benefits. Sunlight and the warmth of the sun are cheering and life-giving, and as creatures of earth we are drawn by them. Equally, careless exposure to the sun can be dangerous. So it is, at the most basic level, with prayer. Mental acknowledgement of that which is beyond our understanding, which for convenience—sometimes almost blasphemously casual convenience—we may term 'God', arises out of a deeper, more primitive experiential level of being. Prayer is a gift of the 'Sun of righteousness' (Mal. 4:2), freely given to all who turn from the arrogance and evildoing, the pretence and perversity, that come so naturally to us as human beings. It is a gift we become open to receiving once we are able to acknowledge within ourselves that 'fear' of the transcendent that is our most primal awareness of life.[30]

*

In a plane attempting to land in dire weather conditions, in an earthquake, under enemy fire, or in any other extreme situation, even people with a robust scepticism or contempt for religious faith can find themselves offering some kind of prayer. This might subsequently be dismissed as a shameful moment of weakness, repudiated in the name of intellectual integrity. But is intellectual integrity the most important aspect of our humanity? Is that what

---

[29] A plea to Jesus by the father of a child suffering fits, desperate for his son to be healed.
[30] Cf. 'fear of the Lord', as discussed above in 'The Spectre Unmasked'.

energizes us, inspires creativity, gives us joy, makes life worth living? Should we not rather ask what it is that fires intellectual activity and gives value to integrity?

Religion is commonly disparaged as a crutch for those who lack the moral or imaginative strength to face life without some confected mental-emotional support. One answer to this might be that this criticism itself suggests a degree of complacency and limited awareness of the diversity and full potentiality of life's horrors and ecstasies. A less contentious and perhaps more Christian answer might be that, yes, we are weak and need support—if you have a broken leg you need a crutch. But with that support we can live a fuller life. It is Christian belief that within every human being there is a fallibility, a weakness, a brokenness which most of us, for most of our lives, do our best to ignore or hide. Organized religion claims and aspires to be a whole-life system that does not only comfort and support, but also challenges and extends our boundaries. Reflecting our fallibility as human beings, it is inevitably far from what it should be. Nevertheless, in this respect it is no different from any other human enterprise.

Religion might be a human-confected system, but so is language itself, and self-aware consciousness evolved through language. It is through constructs of the mind and spirit, grounded in experiential reality, that we are able to recognize our limitedness, the fracturedness of humankind—and in that recognition, experience its defining edge, the comprehending transcendence that at once both stretches and exceeds our limitedness.

*

Many who tick the 'no religion' box on a questionnaire would insist that 'no religion' does not mean no spiritual life. The traditional language and practices of institutional religion may not speak to them, but the basic sense that there is 'more to life', a sense of wonder and common humanity, even a sense of some 'higher power', remains widely shared.

It is far from clear that Jesus had any intention of founding a new religion. He criticized the religious establishment of his day, but was a worshipper in synagogue and temple, and a reformer rather than a revolutionary—although his teaching was certainly felt as threatening and revolutionary by the authorities.[31] He speaks of faith not in terms of dogmatic articles of belief, but of relationship, and of hunger and thirst (e.g. John 6:35), realization of healing as bodily cure yet also something more (e.g. Luke 17:12–19), and life as more than 'all the kingdoms of the world and their glory' (Matt. 4:8). In other words, faith is not a cerebral passion or discrete experience of a 'soul' separate from the body, but part of the weft of our material and psycho-emotional being. For it to develop to its fullest it normally requires the support, guidance and nurture of a consciously articulated belief system or corporate social orthodoxy, but in its raw state, so to speak, it is not dependent on such a structure.

> God is love,
> and those who abide in love abide in God,
> and God abides in them. (1 John 4:16)

*

The technology of modern medical care may keep us alive when, in the not too distant past, we would have died, but it does not in itself make life worth living. It enables us to enjoy a better quality of life in old age, but does not itself deliver that quality of life. Quality of life is a spiritual matter—not in the narrow sense of something non-physical, an ethereal otherness, but in a holistic sense, involving our whole being, *psyche* and *soma*, our physical body and our inner world of intuition, thoughts, emotions, hopes and conscious and unacknowledged fears.

Important in such an understanding of 'quality of life' is the energizing focus, challenge and inner liberation of prayer and the more general, more diffuse meditative state of prayerfulness, which today is probably more widespread than prayer in the strict sense.

---

[31] Matt. 5:17, 'I have come not to abolish, but to fulfil.'

Most commonly perhaps, prayer is seen as a request for supernatural help, whether for an all-clear scan or a punt on a horse, regardless of any moral consideration. For those with a specific religious faith, prayer is an address to a deity or deities, or an intention toward spiritual perfection, defined by the terminology of that faith, with its content and forms shaped accordingly. Meanwhile for those who struggle with the notion of deity conceived, however subtly, as a Supreme Being 'up there', one way of re-thinking prayer might be as an opening of one's self, in an unforced spirit of joy or honest struggle, to the unknowable source and end of all that is. Prayerfulness more generally could be thought of as the dynamic relationship and integration of our ego-self with the external world known to us through sensory, intuited and conceptual experience and moral sentiment. It is how some people describe their experience of, for instance, the practice of a craft, concentration on a hobby, or simply walking.

However defined, prayer is implicit acknowledgement that we, as autonomous individuals, are subject to, or co-operate with, energies with which our will engages yet which are at the same time beyond our control. This acknowledgement in turn releases new energies and experience of wholeness within us. By contrast, when we resort to prayer in the hope of gaining control, achieving status or enrichment, we fall into superstition. True prayer is not conditional on its 'working'. It cannot be instrumentalized. It is an act of unconditional honesty, of non-transactional trust.

> We do not live to ourselves, and we do not die to ourselves. If we live, we live to the Lord, and if we die, we die to the Lord; so then, whether we live or whether we die, we are the Lord's. (Rom. 14:7–8)

Of course we want prayer to 'work'. But one of the perennial issues of prayer is whether and how prayer is 'answered'. The classic response of those with faith is that God answers our prayers, but maybe not always in the way we want; God may have some other purpose for us, which as yet we cannot discern. That response may be correct, but for somebody at a time of agonizing hurt and searching, it probably does little to remedy the bitterness and anger that all too naturally arise from the sense that prayer has not been heard. 'Correct' answers spoken in the wrong spirit cease to be entirely correct. They are generally more for the benefit of the person giving the answer than for the one struggling with physical and spiritual pain. Some people will certainly, in their struggle, engage furiously in philosophical and theological argument. But when that is the case it remains vital, even within the technicalities of debate, to be attentive to the pain they are fighting. Simply offering right theology to someone on the edge of despair is like proposing vintage wine to someone dying of thirst. A sip of water is what is needed. A little love.

It may be that music and poetry are better channels for transmitting this love, because they convey the ferocity of emotions and the tangle of complex, conflictual feelings loosed by grief and the jolting realization of one's own finality. Although not usually in themselves prayer, a poem or piece of music can open the heart and mind, soothe and uplift, in a way that conventional words rarely can. In making allowance for the irrational and, through sound, rhythm and crafted structure, creating space for the extremes and contradictions of our emotional and spiritual life, they resensitize us to the mystery of language and the revivifying power of human creativity. At a time of life when the prospect of death and the reality of unbearable loss make us humiliatingly conscious of the failing of our human capabilities, they can induce in us a lightness of spirit that is intrinsically prayerful.

> And you, my father, there on the sad height,
> Curse, bless, me now with your fierce tears, I pray.
> Do not go gentle into that good night.
> Rage, rage against the dying of the light.[32]

Dylan Thomas's poem is hardly one of resigned serenity, yet the rhymes and inner contradictions create a tautness that achieves remarkable, paradoxical coherence. It conveys a humanity that does not shy from the deep tensions within its psyche. The juxtaposition of

---

[32] Dylan Thomas , from the villanelle 'Do Not Go Gentle into That Good Night' written for his father.

curse/bless and the imperative to 'rage' against a 'dying' that leads to a night identified as 'good', express an emotional openness to illogicality, a fundamental level of universal humanity, of which much conventional Christian writing is overly fearful. As we confront the inevitable moment of our own 'going', it is only when we accept our humanity as it is that we can discover the blessedness of prayer. In Dylan Thomas's poem there is a refusal to abandon the fight against cheap religious 'gentleness'. For all his atheism, his struggle has something of the stubbornness of Jacob's all-night wrestling with the angel.[33]

*

Emotional honesty is the level of Christ's humanity. It is a prerequisite of prayer. Not an intellectual matter, it may come to us in an instant of recognition, perhaps through a word of comfort or a silence of understanding, or may gradually grow as we sense the ineluctable progress of our condition. Perhaps it is no more than a state of utter sincerity vis-à-vis the known, the felt and the unknowable in our lives.

This honesty requires *inter alia* a recognition of ultimate existential powerlessness—in which, however, the very act of cognition is negation of powerlessness. Within that negation, the specific experience of prayer comes through a sense that the energy of life and the cosmos are somehow wholly present, within us, part of us, and that we participate in it. It is Christ's presence beside us, the kingdom within, the life of life itself.

> Great Father of glory, pure Father of light,
> ... O help us to see
> 'tis only the splendour of light hideth thee.[34]

*

---

[33] Gen. 32:22–31.
[34] Walter Chalmers Smith, from the hymn 'Immortal, Invisible, God only Wise'.

Philosophy and theology can, over time, have healing power. The prison writings of the late-Roman Christian Platonist philosopher Boethius, *The Consolation of Philosophy*, were hugely influential throughout the Middle Ages and beyond. When faced with the precariousness and brutality of life, Wisdom can bring a degree of serenity, a steadiness against the cosmic inner chaos of a life crisis.

Thus returning to the question of why God seems not to answer some prayers, despite their being sincerely offered and for a clearly good cause such as the saving of a life or righting of an injustice—ultimately, philosophically, we have to accept that our questioning is itself grounded in the wider context of the unknowability of why we exist in the first place. Our very ability to question and to accept or reject faith is beyond our capacity to comprehend. Probably the best we can do is attribute it to our innate, evolved faculty of reason. However, it is beyond the power of rational descriptive understanding to account for itself. Ultimate understanding belongs only to God. We cannot know why some prayers appear to be answered and some not. But we know that God is knowable through a certain relationship of love that we call belief. Now if God invariably answered prayer in the way that the person praying wished, we would effectively be *obliged* to believe. It would be perverse not to believe in something that demonstrably 'worked'. Hence our freedom to believe or not would be abolished. But a loving God, by definition, will not coerce us into belief.

Such logic-chopping can have consolatory value. Yet in the end the power of God's love, revealed in the incarnate world-structuring Logos, is beyond logic. In an everyday context prayer may be understood as a human plea for particular outcomes and, in the context of a life-limiting condition, as a source of healing, empowerment and comfort. Yet these aspects of prayer are themselves outcomes of a deeper prior experience—however imperfectly understood—of prayer as an unlocking of the heart, and entry into the inner sanctum of our being where our most private, perhaps hitherto unrecognized thoughts and emotions are lodged.[35] We may not be able to, or may

---

[35] Cf. Matt. 6:6.

not wish to, put this into words. But it is the deepest experience of a relational way of being that involves self-surrender and self-discovery, thankfulness, compassion and reorientation of life.

> Thou mastering me
> God! giver of breath and bread;
> World's strand, sway of the sea;
> Lord of living and dead;
> Thou hast bound bones & veins in me, fastened me flesh,
> And after it almost unmade, what with dread,
> Thy doing: and dost thou touch me afresh?
> Over again I feel thy finger and find thee.
>
> I did say yes
> O at lightning and lashed rod;
> Thou heardst me truer than tongue confess
> Thy terror, O Christ, O God;
> Thou knowest the walls, altar and hour and night:
> The swoon of a heart that the sweep and the hurl of thee trod
> Hard down with a horror of height:
> And the midriff astrain with leaning of, laced with fire of stress.
>
> The frown of his face
> Before me, the hurtle of hell
> Behind, where, where was a, where was a place?
> I whirled out wings that spell
> And fled with a fling of the heart to the heart of the Host.
> My heart, but you were dovewinged, I can tell,
> Carrier-witted, I am bold to boast,
> To flash from the flame to the flame then, tower from the grace to the grace.[36]

---

[36] Gerard Manley Hopkins, opening stanzas of 'The Wreck of the Deutschland'.

THE NECESSITY OF PRAYER

Illness and bereavement can either stimulate prayer or, at least apparently, crush it. Finding that one is no longer able to pray, for whatever reason, is a desolating experience. But when life has been radically changed, it is impossible to continue in one's inner life as if nothing was different. Sometimes when faced with the prospect or presence of death people are burdened with an expectation that their faith as hitherto practised should be able to carry them through. They feel guilty, or are made to feel guilty, if they seem to be faltering in faith, not praying 'hard enough'. This can be very damaging. In all probability what may be required is a new, perhaps radically new, understanding of faith and way of prayer, accommodating the new reality of emotional wounds and bodily limitations. Adapting mentally and emotionally takes time and can create uncertainty and disorientation. Yet letting go of the old and allowing the way ahead to reveal itself, rather than battling to maintain at all costs a previous discipline of prayer or spiritual understanding, can be a process of enrichment and deepening of spiritual life, regardless of whether we are progressing toward healing or the end of our life. Moulding the space in which our being finds realization, material circumstances are, we discover, integral to the nature of prayer, and prayer is integral to continued fullness of living.

Meanwhile, sadly, 'life circumstances' can also lead to agonizing doubt and loss of faith. The painful, long drawn-out suffering of a loved one, or the death of a child, can destroy belief in an all-powerful loving God. Natural disasters and wars similarly prompt intractable questions that can bring religious convictions crashing down.

Loss of faith can lead in various directions. For some it may actually result in a sense of liberation and discovery of new intellectual possibilities. In such cases the crucial thing is the 'fruits' of this inward change—'by their fruits you will know them.' (Matt. 7:18–20). For others loss of faith may result in a sense of emptiness and directionlessness which can sometimes turn out to be a 'wilderness experience' through which, miraculously, a more profound faith emerges. For yet others it can lead to bitterness, uncritical cynicism, and emotional entrapment in the experience of loss. The problem here is deeper than one of simple intellectual conviction. Rejection of faith can paradoxically lead to an unconscious dependence on that which has been rejected, to a sense of identity defined more by what has been rejected than by any positive new understanding of life—a kind of inversion of the spirit, a belief in a force of malevolence within the world, which only the power of the compassion of Christ can remedy. In such instances, rather than trying to persuade people back to faith by force of argument, probably the best we can do is to hold them lovingly in prayer, and as far as possible retain their friendship, while accepting that friendships too can die.

A further category of loss of faith is perhaps the most common. Many who find their faith undermined by the arbitrariness and scale of evil and suffering in the world find it nevertheless impossible to accept that creation's equally manifest beauty, ordered complexity, and goodness are the random product of blind forces that merely *are*. Despite everything, they are unwilling to believe that impersonal existence ('it's just the way things are') can adequately account for the experiential reality of consciousness and personhood. Along with intellectual doubts, they continue to allow, at a holistic human level, the possibility of some kind of benevolent Providence.

For doubter and believer alike, however, the messiness and unfairness of death in so many instances raise in the starkest form the question of how a benevolent all-powerful Providence can permit suffering and injustice. Attempts (known technically as theodicy, and described as optimistic) to 'justify' God or philosophically resolve this dilemma are met by more pessimistic 'realist' views.

The struggle to reconcile the manifest goodness in creation with, at the same time, seemingly pointless suffering and evil, plays out in public debate as well as in individuals' lives. In 1755 the destruction of the city of Lisbon by a massive earthquake, in which over 30,000 people died, led to intense argument among philosophers and theologians about the nature of God, with Voltaire famously moving to a more 'pessimistic' outlook. Their successors two centuries later, including, as we have seen, Tillich in *The Courage to Be*, grappled with the spiritual implications of the human-devised and executed Holocaust and the atomic bomb.

A different, less conceptual approach to the problem of how we can retain faith in the goodness of God despite the monstrous evils that so often seem to dominate is offered by the Jewish Existentialist thinker Martin Buber (1878–1965). In his book *I and Thou*,[37] written in the aftermath of the First World War — a cataclysm that put in question the entire 'project' of Christian Europe and enlightened science — he advocates unmediated holistic engagement *with* reality and meaningfulness as a vital counterweight to philosophical discussion *of* them. Empirical perception and analysis (described as a relationship of 'I and It') are contrasted with an attitude of personal, living interaction with reality, described as 'I and Thou'. The former necessitates observational detachment (reality on the mortuary slab, as it is sometimes disparagingly called). The latter is the holistic, experiential dynamic of organic lived perception.

Before looking at how Buber's ideas might be helpful in reconciling belief in an all-powerful good God with those voices within us that cry out against that God's apparent indifference to injustice and cruelty, we need to reflect briefly on the title-word 'Thou'. In current English the intimate second-person singular word for 'you', has fallen out of use, and sounds archaic. The equivalent 'du' in the German original, however, is still a completely normal everyday word. The Anglophone reader thus has to make an imaginative effort

---

[37] *Ich und Du*, published in German in 1923. First English translation 1937, later translated by Walter Kaufmann (Charles Scribner's Sons, 1970).

to recover the sense of unforced, intimate directness conveyed by the I-Thou relationship.[38]

While we necessarily experience the world through sensation at an I-It level, experience itself has a holistic subjectivity that engages every part of our being. I-It extracts information from the 'other' for the benefit of the self. I-Thou affirms both the self and the 'other' in a unity of encounter. Oscillating between these two modes of relationship, we hold in tension the realities of the world on the one hand and, on the other, the greater reality that actually empowers perception, reason, questioning, and value judgements.

Unlike some forms of dualism, it does not present matter — the I-It world in general — in negative terms. Evil, for Buber, consists in lack of relationship. Following his insights, it might be said that loss of faith occurs when the objective facts of cruelty and arbitrary death are seen as independently existent, decoupled from the ultimate truth of our existence as holistic, non-autonomous beings dependent on a transcendent value source that enables us to recognize good and evil in the first place.

The I-Thou relationship connects every element of creation since all existence is informed with the will of the living God. In the I-It world of necessity and function we see things as living or dead, animate or inanimate. By contrast I-Thou sees that all that is, including mortality, exists in relation to a living source. I-It grapples with problems of understanding; I-Thou is realization of what understanding is. I-Thou always ultimately points to the divine. And the ultimate I-Thou relationship is directly with God.

Crucially, for Christians that ultimate relationship is through the Logos made flesh in Christ Jesus — in whom also the world of I-It,

---

[38] It should be noted that the same effort is required when we say the Lord's Prayer in its traditional seventeenth-century form. The sense of close familiarity in the second-person singular verb form, 'art in heaven', has become lost — indeed the archaic language creates a formal distance that is almost the exact opposite of the original intimacy of 'art'. For most of us, the loss of meaning is even greater in the opening of the *Nunc dimittis*, 'Lord, now lettest thou thy servant depart in peace'.

historical fact and the crucifying dilemmas of faith, integrity, and vulnerability, is taken into the Godhead. When our faith is shaken by the remorseless challenges of evil and the seeming indifference of a remote divinity, *Deus absconditus*, it is to the crucified Christ that we need to turn. Rather than seek redemption through the I-It world of philosophical debate, theodicy, and rational ethics, necessary as these are, we need to recognize that these are themselves redeemable only through a wholly other level of experience. They are ultimately meaningful only through direct relationship with the Word, the Thou of personal encounter with 'the Alpha and the Omega, the beginning and the end' (Rev. 22:13) in the world of birth and death, pain and grief, joy and love, conditionality and incompleteness in which Jesus calls us to discipleship.

How does this encounter happen in practice? How do we advocate for such an approach to those who, appalled by the brute evil in the world, find it impossible to continue believing in an all-powerful good God, yet also impossible wholly to renounce belief in the ultimate value of Life? Above all surely we need to advocate for courageous openness to the possibility that beauty, justice, love, and goodness have incontestable reality, even though they will for ever evade definitive description. Properties of the divine Logos, ultimately beyond discursive knowledge, they can in the end only be *lived*, through relationships spiritually conformed to love of God and love of neighbour (cf. Mark 12:29–31). And such relationships, characterized by compassion and service, and bearing the fruit of the Spirit—'love, joy, peace, patience, kindness, generosity, faithfulness, gentleness, and self-control' (Gal. 5.22–3)—are fed and sustained by prayer—in its broadest sense, as discussed in the previous chapter.

For those for whom formal prayer can be helpful, I offer the prayer below in the spirit of I-Thou, second-person direct address, either as preparation for deeper, more contemplative prayer, or as a general self-dedication to whatever good purpose God intends in our lives.

Blessed Lord, who are all in all –
Open my eyes to see the day of your glory;
My ears to hear the song of the Divine Word;
My heart to be moved in the power of the Spirit;
My mouth to speak your praise;
My hands to serve you, as you give me strength,
Till my last breath.

*

Those of us fortunate enough to have access to advanced health care are in danger of taking it for granted as 'normal'. Harbouring this largely unconscious assumption, we become depressed at glitches in the system, angry at its inevitable failures. It is salutary to remind ourselves that most people in the world have a very different 'normal'. In situations where there is minimal medical provision and where death is less 'professionalized', people cannot but be more acutely aware of their mortality. Traditional remedies and prayer are at least accessible and thus a correspondingly more significant part of everyday life.

For the disciples of Jesus, in a society under military occupation, where angels and demons determined health as much as pre-modern remedies, and 'in the midst of life we are in death', prayer had an essential practical function. It was a source of strength, hope and dignity in a situation of subordination, powerlessness and instability. Prayer has a completely functional importance which, when life is going smoothly, we tend not to appreciate, but which at crisis time can be a vital resource. When our body is traumatized or taken over by destructive cells or hostile microbiological forces, we need to meet the problem with all practical means. Giving praise and glory to God and praying with tears and thanksgiving, with all our heart, mind, soul and strength (see Mark 12:30), is to observe the first commandment of life. When the disciples asked their 'Rabbi' how they should pray, he gave them a concise template in what has come to be known as the Lord's Prayer. Faced with a potentially terminal disease or life emergency, it is not just a question of praying for a successful outcome to treatment, although that is of course central. Prayer also has a broader function. It is a means of aligning one's whole being with the suffering inherent in the human condition; and in complementarity with professional medical care, with the humane intentions of those who minister to others. It is an offering of oneself in trust, body and spirit, not simply as a patient to be treated, but in unspoken blessing upon our own carers' humanity and skills, in a joint enterprise of life.

Where medical care is less advanced, this 'functional' level of prayer is more evident. Fear of death and grief at loss are no less intense for being more 'normal' in less developed societies. But when social support structures are unreliable or lacking, the imperatives of living without a safety net and the gruelling practicalities of adjustment to loss of an income earner are all the more pressing. Prayer and blessings have correspondingly all the more significance. Dependence on wider family can lead to strong familial networks, but also to further vulnerability and exploitation of the dependent. In many parts of the world, religious adherence and prayer, while sometimes problematic, even abusive, are a vital part of a societal support system. Prayer in such situations tends to be more 'applied', collective and socially visible than in societies where welfare provision, one-to-one bereavement- and mental-health counselling, and individualistic culture, reduce its role to one amongst an array of consumer-choice therapy options. Advanced healthcare brings many results for which we should be grateful. Yet for all those benefits there is a loss of something essential to wellbeing when the spiritual dimension of life is reduced to a marginal optional extra. Often remarked upon by visitors to the affluent world from poorer countries, is a curious lack of joy.

*

> The healing of his seamless dress
> is by our beds of pain;
> we touch him in life's throng and press,
> and we are whole again.[39]

These lines refer to the Gospel account of the woman who pushed through the 'throng and press' of people surrounding Jesus to touch the fringe of his cloak, to receive healing from a seemingly incurable medical condition that rendered her ritually unclean (Luke 8:43–8). Her 'prayer' was of the most primitive kind—simply to reach out and physically touch. Does Jesus tick her off for being superstitious? No. He accepts her faith for what it is, demands no assent to any credo, imposes no conditions on the miracle.

The writer of that hymn verse conflates that story with the description in St John's Gospel of Christ's robe, which was woven all in a single piece (John 19:23). The four lines together contrast the indoor confinement of suffering with the outdoor bustle of the street, the privacy of the one and the public context of the other. An important element of the latter, however, is that the woman wished to remain anonymous. Her condition was shaming and she dreaded losing the privacy that was her only solace for her misfortune. But Jesus draws her out from that protective anonymity. Healing does not remain in the private one-to-one space into which we tend to retreat when living with implacable sorrow or incurable disease. It is a call to full participation in life.

Jesus condemns the ostentatious public piety of the scribes and pharisees, and tells his disciples, 'whenever you pray, go into your room and shut the door and pray to your Father who is in secret.' (Matt. 6:6). Yet that 'secret' place is intentional, not just a shrinking from the world due to a sense of 'uncleanness' or resentment at being unfairly marked out by fate. Paradoxically it connects us with the world, because every single person has that same 'room' within them, granting access to the universal gaze of Divine Love. In the 'secrecy' of God's particular love

---

[39] John Greenleaf Whittier, from the hymn 'Immortal Love, Forever Full'.

for us, as the unique individual each one of us is, we are one with every other uniquely loved human being. That uniqueness is what we have in common. It is what makes each one of us part of the social body, the 'seamless' whole that is our essential human nature.

*

Death is remorselessly not private. Quite simply we cannot dispose of our own body. The irrational shame that attaches to that loss of autonomy, and to whatever renders our mortality visible to the world, goes very deep. Overcoming it can be hard. Public figures who announce they have a terminal condition are applauded for their courage. Balancing the public and private elements of our life is never easy. Part of the work of formal prayer is to mediate in a loving way between the intensely personal and the public, the emotional and psychological reality of our personal condition, its abnormality, and the normality of death as an impartial matter of fact.

Meanwhile, amid the tedium and restlessness, the sheer business of being unwell, it can be a huge relief to go into that inner 'room' of the heart, close the door, and simply be alone with the One who made us and knows us better than we know ourselves. To begin to pray, we need do no more than reach out, in whatever emotional or mental way the desire takes us, to touch 'the fringe of the cloak' of the Divine, the source of life. As we take that risk, of venturing out of the secure space of our autonomous individual self into the uncontrollable 'throng and press' of common humanity to which we each uniquely contribute, we sense a radical new dimension to being. The powerful negativity of our 'rage' against 'the dying of the light' becomes redirected toward the goodness of 'that good night'. What flows from this reorientation of the heart need not be voiced or even consciously articulated, yet, emerging simultaneously from the core of our personal identity and the unfathomable vastness of reality 'out there', it is a cry of life accompanying birth into a new relationship to the world.

*

Ill health can be a battle with long stretches of boredom, but also times of busyness and worry. The following prayer might be suitable for the morning of a day when an operation or procedure has been scheduled. Or simply, adapted appropriately, when visits from doctors and nurses or carers will require your full attention. Or when the practicalities of self-care absorb all your energy.

> O Lord! thou knowest how busy I must be this day:
> if I forget thee, do not thou forget me.[40]

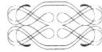

---

[40] Jacob Astley, First Baron Hastings, before the battle of Edgehill, 1642, in Sir Philip Warwick, *Memoires of the Reign of King Charles I. Containing the most remarkable Occurrences of that Reign ... to the Happy Restauration of King Charles II* (Printed for Ri. Chiswell, 1701), 229.

KNOWING WE ARE NOT ALONE

> Its [the soul's] Love is a dominion greater than that which Adam had in Paradise: and yet the fruition of it is but solitary. We need spectators, and other diversities of friends and lovers, in whose souls we might likewise dwell, and with whose beauties we might be crowned, and entertained. In all whom we can dwell exactly, and be present with them fully. Lest therefore the other depths and faculties of our souls should be desolate and idle, they also are created to entertain us. And as in many mirrors we are so many other selves, so are we spiritually multiplied when we meet ourselves more sweetly, and live again in other persons.[41]

Love is the experience of union that makes our existence as physically separate entities a source of delight, creative complementarity, unreplicable harmony. By contrast those experiences in life, most notably bereavement and the approach of our own death, which drive home the separateness of our individual existence, can fill us with a sense of isolation, of abandonment even by God, that can be terrifying. We find ourselves suddenly on our own, face-to-face with the emptiness of the cosmos. In Pascal's famous evocation of a Godless void in his *Pensées*: *Le silence éternel de ces espaces infinis m'effraie*—'the eternal silence of these infinite spaces frightens me', he is referring to 'the infinite immensity of spaces whereof I am ignorant, and which know me not' in relation to 'the little space which I fill'.[42]

People sometimes cope with such experiences through evasive, compensatory busyness and sociability, sometimes through withdrawal into a shell of self-isolation. In certain states it can be difficult even

---

[41] Thomas Traherne, *Centuries*, II.70. Continuation of the passage quoted in the section 'Body and Soul', p. 18 above.
[42] Pascal, *Pensées*, Fragment 233.

to want to move on. 'My soul refuses comfort.' (Ps. 77:2). To accept tragedy and strive for happiness in changed circumstances may feel like a betrayal of what had been before. 'Survivor guilt' can be difficult to cope with. To envisage living with drastic new constraints after a major accident or life-changing surgery may require a total mental re-orientation of attitude to disability and assumptions about human worth. It takes courage to embark on the path of reconciliation with life in its new configuration, and to persist, whether toward one's final days or into a daunting future, despite setbacks and further hurt. There is tension between the need on the one hand to accept limits realistically, and on the other to defy those limits, push beyond them, not be defined by them.

Gradually, like strengthening of muscles, confidence grows and establishes the ground for re-engagement with the world. In this often lengthy process the support, encouragement and companionship of others are crucial. 'The infinite immensity of spaces whereof I am ignorant, and which know me not' becomes a populated, humanly-navigable space through the love, friendship and skills of family, friends and neighbours, those who have gone through similar experiences, and professionals committed to helping their patients discover new hope and accommodation with whatever the future may hold. This network or community of fellow human beings affords us a glimpse of 'the communion of saints', the transcendent reality of the Body of Christ.[43]

*

Some people wish not to talk about health problems or sadnesses, however serious. This might be an attempt to avoid having to face the disturbing, frightening reality, or alternatively a courageous decision not to burden and depress others. Either way, it can result in dissimulation, and create difficulties, both practical and emotional, for others. For many, perhaps most people, talking about death and the mental

---

[43] See the Apostles' Creed, and e.g. 1 Cor. 12:12–27.

and emotional impact of a terminal diagnosis or bereavement or trauma is important. It is part of the process of finding a new equilibrium, to enable us to embrace the future in a positive, even happy way. It is also helpful in preparing family, friends, and associates, so that they have time to adjust to what will be a major event in their lives.

Opportunities for such conversations, beyond practical matters, are relatively few, however. The emotional impact on family and friends can sometimes make dispassionate, undramatic discussion almost impossible. Professional therapy is usually expensive and does not suit everyone. Church congregations may provide support, but this can be rather hit-and-miss. Bible study groups can provide a more structured setting for discussing big issues, with room for including personal experience, but the focus will not primarily be on the personal. Much depends on the pastoral sensitivity of the leader and the collective sensitivity of the group. Hospices and palliative carers offer wonderful volunteer and skilled professional support, but unfortunately are under-resourced and not always available to everyone. Local community organizations and online and social media support groups can offer invaluable help, and 'Death Cafés' have become increasingly popular.

> At a Death Café people drink tea, eat cake and discuss death. Our aim is to increase awareness of death to help people make the most of their (finite) lives.[44]

People publicize their own health condition to fundraise for charity and raise awareness of unfamiliar health challenges through stunts and media platforms. These can generate a tremendous sense of solidarity and common purpose, as well as significant amounts of money. In all these ways our need for 'spectators, and other diversities of friends and lovers', to use Traherne's phrase, is met and celebrated.

*

---

[44] https://deathcafe.com/ (accessed 18.11.24).

It is remarkable how human solidarity and common purpose tend most often to crystallize around tragedy and death. Self-interested competition engenders solidarity, but of a compartmentalized and precarious kind. Even sport, which is essentially friendly, can be vitiated by tribal loyalties and financial interests, as nationalism and commercialization around the Olympic and major league competitions vividly demonstrate. The arts, meanwhile, achieve their greatest expression when there is reference, even if oblique, to the pain and tragedy of life and the power of the human spirit to overcome these. The unifying force here, and ultimately also the foundation stone of justice, is compassion.

The supreme emblem of redemptive unity through tragedy and death and the exposure of injustice is the Cross of Christ. Although appropriated by 'Christianity' in all its glorious, debased, life-giving, corrupted and corrupting manifestations, Christ's compassion on the Cross is for all people throughout all time. The Cross is not just for the 'true believer'. Maximus the Confessor describes Christ's death on the Cross as 'a judgement of judgement.'[45] It represents physically and cosmically 'the breadth and length and height and depth' (Eph. 3.18–19) of God's love for us and the whole of creation.

> Jesus has shown us in his own person all the fullness of life offered on the tree ... This tree of celestial dimensions rises up from the earth to heaven, an eternal plant deeply rooted in heaven and earth, the foundation of the universe, assembling together all the diversity of humankind, fastened by invisible nails of the Spirit, so that its links with the divine power may never again be broken ...[46]

For the early Church, Christ is, as the Orthodox theologian Olivier Clément writes,

> the truly cosmic Man who transfigures the universe: 'Henceforward all is filled with light, the heavens, the earth, and even hell', according

---

[45] *Questions to Thalassius,* 43, cited in Olivier Clément, *The Roots of Christian Mysticism: Text and Commentary* (New City, 2015), 49.

[46] Anonymous fourth-century *Homily for Easter,* cited in Clément, *The Roots of Christian Mysticism,* 48.

to the Easter liturgy in the Byzantine rite. To be crucified in Christ is to die to one's own death in order to enter into the sacrifice that restores wholeness.[47]

Far from being confined to the individual affective experience that modern Christians, especially in the Western tradition, generally take to be the salvific work of Jesus through his Passion, death and Resurrection, the Cross has universal objective efficacy. The anonymous fourth-century author of the Easter Homily quoted above writes,

> There is little doubt that the whole world would have been annihilated ... if Jesus in his majesty had not breathed forth the divine Spirit, saying, 'Father, into thy hands I commit my spirit' (Luke 23:46). And when the Divine Spirit ascended, the universe was given life, strength, and stability.[48]

In this understanding of God's redeeming love in the Word made flesh, restored creation has no room for the desperate isolation and loneliness that afflicts us in our current mortal condition. All are embraced and united in the Body of Christ. Despising the shame of the Cross (Heb. 12:2), Jesus exposes the injustice, skewed values and inhumanity of conventional social hierarchies. The self-righteous proprieties that create a world of peeping, hypocritical solitarinesses are shown up for what they are. Discovering, through the self-giving compassion of others, that in fact one is not alone, that in all kinds of ways bodily frailty and the prospect of death create new forms of human solidarity, opens up new dimensions of love. No longer defined by the existential separateness that is the necessary condition of human love between individuals, this new level of solidarity exists as a transcendent fellowship of simple humanity, actualized in down-to-earth individual relationships. It is recognition of some common factor within us all that has inexpressible dignity, speaks of ultimate value, is lovable.

*

---

[47] Clément, *The Roots of Christian Mysticism*, 47.
[48] *Homily for Easter*, in Clément, *The Roots of Christian Mysticism*, 49.

The sense of aloneness when faced with the prospect of death is often overlain with other feelings, anxiety about the bodily process of dying, the possibility of uncontrollable pain, anger and a sense of unfairness, grief at the cutting off of a young life or deprivation of anticipated future career or pleasures such as seeing children or grandchildren grow up. Arguments over inheritance can already have blown up or be brewing. The frustrations and humiliations of becoming dependent and losing control of physical functions create a sense of loss of dignity, which can lead to shame, inner self-isolation and self-rejection. But perhaps underlying all is an unarticulated awareness of having to encounter death purely for oneself. No-one can die for us. Our birth was in some sense a joint activity between our mother and ourselves. Our dying will, at an organic level, involve only us.

Only redemptive love can break through the multiple defences of this aloneness. As discussed above, once we find the courage to accept our need for care, we open ourselves up to the exponentially greater experience of redemptive love, through the simple attention and kindnesses of those who offer companionship and social and medical help, especially when family and friendship networks are lacking. Love can also be communicated through cultural contacts and relationships, and the knowledge that others are 'rooting' for us. In all such interactions the healing grace of Christ, the cosmic Word, is implicit. In the most profound way, however, redemptive love is experienced explicitly through prayer and eucharistic fellowship.

Sharing in Holy Communion, we share not only in the Body of a particular congregation, however large or small, but in 'the communion of saints' throughout all ages, who are as integral to the Body as those still living. In Christ there is no division of time. In the remembering of Christ through shared bread and wine we are spiritually one in the mystical Body of the whole of redeemed humanity. Drawing on the image of the Body of the Church and its identification with the Body of Christ in St Paul's first letter to the early Christian community in Corinth (1 Cor. 12), the fourth-century theologian Gregory of Nyssa writes:

In our body the activity of any one of our senses communicates sensation to the whole of the organism joined to that member. It is the same for humanity as a whole, which forms, so to speak, a single living being: the resurrection of one member extends to all, and that of a part to the whole, by virtue of the cohesion and unity of human nature.[49]

The solitariness of our existence as discrete individuals is transformed by this connection, both bodily and spiritual, with brothers and sisters in Christ around the world, living in all kinds of different circumstances, and with those other saints, the great 'cloud of witnesses' (Heb. 12:1), our brothers and sisters in the heavenly realms.

In intercessory remembrance, voiced or unvoiced, we are in communion with those around the world who are also at the threshold of death at the present time—particularly those living without the anaesthetics, drugs and medical facilities that we in the developed world so take for granted. Such intercession can help relativize our own suffering, indeed even be a kind of blessing, to nourish greater compassion in our thinking and being. Holding before us the Cross of Christ, remembering those who at this precise moment, wherever it may be, are suffering imprisonment, abuse and torture, we offer through our own pain an exchange of solidarity that, by faith, has untold potential healing grace.

When housebound, or in hospital, it can be transformative at a very basic psychological level to receive Holy Communion. It is most unfortunate that for some people this, like the sacrament of anointing, is seen as a kind of sending-off ceremony into the hereafter. The *viaticum* (provision for a journey), as it is sometimes called, is indeed part of the last rites of the Church, but equally it is part of the journey of our healing and living. The consecrated host physically connects us with the whole of life. We are no longer confined in our bed or within the four walls of a room, but are filled with remembrance of the wonder of God's world, the companionship of countless saints known and unknown to us, the enjoyment of the angelic worship of

---

[49] *Catechetical Orations*, *32*, cited in Clément, *The Roots of Christian Mysticism*, 47.

heaven, the self-giving love of Christ and the 'Divine Intoxication' of the Spirit.

*

Offering and receiving prayer as part of the communion of saints, we hold each other before God, not as the person we assume or judge others and ourselves to be, but as the person only God ultimately knows each of us to be.

For those in better health who find themselves sitting alongside others in situations of extreme weakness, spoken prayer, best kept simple and brief, may be helpful, indeed life-changing. We cannot know. All we can do is seek to act with love, neither imposing a self-concerned desire to act lovingly, nor requiring any emotional payback. Even people with no religious belief may appreciate it if, unpretentiously, without spiritual flimflam, we wish them God's blessing. Indeed, if we are known as a person of faith, letting someone know that they are in our prayers might be important. Though not sharing our faith, they might still appreciate knowing that we, for whom faith is central, do not exclude them.

For patients, however, there are times when we are unable to focus on the externals of prayer. As death approaches, inevitably the spirit becomes less corporeal. Often a sense of humour and clear-minded intellect continues even as the body becomes ever more of an 'encumbrance' — King Charles II, dying of kidney failure, famously told those at his bedside, 'You must pardon me, gentlemen, for being a most unconscionable time a-dying.' But with increasing physical weakness, the spirit becomes more purely internal. This 'progress' of the soul was evident in the final moments of the life of the saintly seventeenth-century bishop Lancelot Andrewes:

> In the time of his fever and last sickness, besides the often prayers which were read to him, in which he repeated all the parts of the Confession and other petitions with an audible voice, as long as his strength endured, he did — as was well observed by certain tokens in

him—continually pray to himself, though he seemed otherwise to rest or slumber; and when he could pray no longer *voce*—with his voice, yet *oculis et manibus*, 'by lifting up his eyes and hands' he prayed still, and when both voice and eyes and hands failed in their office, then *corde*, 'with his heart', he still prayed, until it pleased God to receive his blessed soul to Himself.[50]

With modern intensive care skills and technology, this 'progress' can, much more commonly than in the past, go in the opposite direction, toward renewed life. From a state where prayer is simply identification with physically continuing to be alive after catastrophic injury and surgery, voice, eyes, hands gradually re-acquire function, however limited—or we come to realize more clearly the drastic loss of faculties. In the battle to adjust to 'a second life', and to face that gift without horror at the crippled or bionic existence that may be our future, the flotsam of a shattered spiritual life can offer something to hold on to.

Keep your mind in hell, and do not despair.[51]

*

Formal prayer may well be beyond our powers of concentration as we negotiate, physically and psychologically, 'the valley of the shadow of death'. There are some whose temperament and life experience enable them to face death with a cheerful stoicism or devil-may-care humour, although they perhaps do not always recognize the support received from others, who may in fact bear some of the emotional burden for them—and cheerfulness or indifference can be a kind of armour-plating against the unsettling demands of the soul.

---

[50] From Bishop John Buckeridge's Sermon at Andrewes' funeral. Quoted in A. E. Burn's introduction to *The Preces Privatae of Lancelot Andrewes* (Methuen & Co Ltd, 1949), xi.

[51] St Silouan the Athonite, *Wisdom from Mount Athos: The Writings of Staretz Silouan, 1866–1938*, ed. Archimandrite Sofroniï (St Vladimir's Seminary Press, 1974), 119.

For some, by contrast, defence against unconscious spiritual demands can take the form of unfocussed rage, resentment, or passive resignation. Such feelings destroy or block the potentially creative and revelatory experiences that the end of life can offer, and confirm in those without faith the futility and deceit of religion. Where acceptance grows, however, and we sense the grace of a life-power beyond anything we could have conceived before,[52] space for new understanding is opened up. Within this space the joy of faith can find expression. Individual words and phrases, perhaps repeated with the regularity of breathing, aloud or silently, can bring healing and comfort. Simple words—'God', 'glory', 'joy', 'help', 'dear Jesus'—can have transformative power.

Healing grace may be for recovery of physical strength and capacities. Or it may be for inner readiness for the approaching completeness of our life's story. A whispered 'Thank you!' can express appreciation simply for the amazing experience of having lived. On one occasion I was told by nurses that the patient to whom I had brought Communion the previous day had died singing. Familiar prayers, especially the Lord's Prayer, are a kind of life raft, with space for all who might wish to come on board. Prayers of confession and forgiveness, assurance of mercy, commendation and blessing, spoken by a minister, with administration of the sacraments of Communion and anointing, bring to the dying not a demand for intellectual acceptance of dogma, but the compassion and promises of Christ in the loving presence of his very Body, the Church. Externals such as the priest's stole, a little crucifix, and well-ironed linen for the Communion, trivial as they are, can also communicate the care of the Body, in the context of rumpled bedding and cluttered bedside table.

At work in the mystery of Church is also the intercessory miracle of the Body. However truncated by circumstances, the holy eucharist is offered in communion with blessed Mary, who knew the agony of

---

[52] Cf. St Anselm's *Proslogion*: 'God is that, than which nothing greater can be conceived.'

witnessing the torture and death of her son, and with the saints and martyrs of every age, and those in our own age with whom we share our common humanity. Receiving the consecrated host, we take into our own wounded and changed body, in silent or voiced prayer, the substance of God's love for the whole world; and commit our future, whatever course it might take, to a new engagement with and celebration of life.

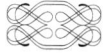

'I HOPE I'LL BE ALIVE WHEN I DIE'

The elderly Yorkshire woman with a twinkle in her eye laughed as she heard herself come out with this phrase. She had already been resuscitated three times, and assured me, 'It's ever so easy dying, you know.' Her words, and giggle, and the twinkle in her eye, have remained with me. She did not mention having had any 'near-death experience' such as others have described after resuscitation from clinical death or catastrophic injury—an out-of-body perspective, a vision of brightness at the end of a tunnel or staircase, an all-pervading sense of serenity and peace, or some form of angelic presence. In fact most people who have had a cardiac arrest and been resuscitated do not report any supernatural experience. My own experience of cardiac arrest (if clinical death can be called an experience, since by definition being dead cannot be *experienced*) was accompanied by no vision: on returning to consciousness I felt, at most, a perplexing blip in my existence, as if a number of frames had been deleted from a film sequence. There was, nevertheless, something different about life. My existence had been, so to speak, ratcheted up a notch.

Re-applying the Yorkshire lady's assurance that dying is 'ever so easy', it is all too 'easy' for us to end up pursuing a kind of half-life, living on automatic pilot, wrapped up in the inessential worries and petty compensations of everyday existence. Like the early Christians in the city of Sardis, in modern day Turkey, we can be outwardly successful yet inwardly empty. 'You have won a name for being alive, yet you are dead,' St John the Divine writes to them in the Book of Revelation. 'Be vigilant, fortify the things that remain that are moribund, for I have not found your works to be fulfilled in the eyes of my God.' (Rev. 3:1–2). Similarly those in the wealthy city of Laodicea, also in modern Turkey, are reprehended for their spiritual complacency:

> The Amen, the witness faithful and true, the origin of God's creation, says these things: I know your works—that you are neither hot nor cold. I would that you were cold or hot. Thus, since you are lukewarm, and neither hot nor cold, I am about to vomit you from my mouth. (Rev. 3:14–16)

Life and death are not constituted wholly by continuation or termination of biological functioning. Such functioning is a *sine qua non* of life in its normal sense, but the values that bestow on physical existence its sacrosanct quality derive from a quite other vision of what it is to live. In his book *Petre Țuțea: Between Sacrifice and Suicide*,[53] the psychiatrist Alexandru Popescu explores the life and thinking of one of the most important Romanian dissidents of the Communist years. Speaking from his long experience of prison and house arrest, Țuțea suggests that we all have a fundamental choice to make in life—that between sacrificial self-giving generosity and self-gratifying acquisitiveness, which amounts to moral suicide. To live in the truest sense is to allow hope and love to govern our lives, rather than greed, fear and expediency. To stay confined within a self focussed on self-preservation and self-advancement is to die spiritually. To live is to be open to the complexity and nuances of human personhood and the infinite diversity and potential of creation, rather than imprisoned in categories of thought and ideology into which reality must be made to fit. It is wisdom over intelligence, understanding over data-accumulation, intercommunication over siloed experience. It is being alive when we die.

Spiritual death can occur in as many ways as physical death. It may be an unnoticed decline into habits of mind and activity that blunt our capacity for joy, or it might be a single 'deal with the devil' that will irrevocably affect one's whole future. In the context of illness, grief, adjustment to a terminal diagnosis, or the need to adapt to drastically-curtailed capacities after life-preserving medical intervention, the temptation to give up on life can be great. At times it may feel the struggle is not worth it. The spirit has gone out of us, and this can in

---

[53] Alexandru Popescu, *Petre Țuțea: Between Sacrifice and Suicide* (Routledge, 2004).

fact hasten physical death. But in all such situations there is also, by the grace of Christ, the possibility of 'a second life', a Lazarus resuscitation (John 11:1–44), brought about by some encounter that brings love and hope into the darkness. Responding to this, however, requires a positive turning away from despair, toward the huge effort of re-emergence into life.

At an everyday level, there is a kind of spiritual death every time we speak or think judgementally of our neighbour; every time we claim or imply credit for ourselves while failing to acknowledge good luck or the contribution of others; every time we close our eyes and heart to others' distress. Daily, in innumerable ways, we experience organic spiritual death. It is how we are as human beings. And it is to counter this that we are exhorted to 'Rejoice always, pray without ceasing, give thanks in all circumstances. For this is God's will toward you in the Anointed One Jesus.' (1 Thess. 5:16–18). This constant prayer in the spirit requires the self-discipline of honest application. It is a sacrificial way of being that works the miracle of ever new life for us, even within the body of our physical and spiritual mortality.

The prayer most commonly associated with the injunction to 'pray without ceasing' is the so-called Jesus Prayer, or Prayer of the Heart.

> Lord Jesus Christ,
> Son of God,
> Have mercy on me.

The last line is often given a penitential emphasis—'Have mercy on me, a sinner', or 'sinner that I am'. The three words of the first line evoke in themselves the fathomless mystery of the Holy Trinity: 'Lord', the authority of being; the Divine Word made flesh in our brother Jesus; the anointing Spirit in the Christ. It is a prayer of simple appeal which, repeated steadily, leads in time to a point at which, according to the traditional formulation, the mind descends into the heart, and words are no longer needed.

To 'pray without ceasing' involves every level of our being, an orientation toward that love that is 'all in all' through every aspect of our lives, our relationships, our respect for our own body and environment, our willing sacrifice of self-regard in favour of the greater vision of love that is the ultimate calling of human existence.

Just as we throw ourselves upon Christ's merciful, loving intercession for us at the right hand of God (cf. Rom. 8:34), we can in turn know Jesus more nearly and love him more dearly[54] through his relatable human nature by the intercession of Mary, his mother. For millions of Christians throughout the world the 'Hail Mary' is a meditative prayer that takes us to the very heart of the communion of saints, bringing untold consolation especially in its repeated petition: 'Holy Mary, Mother of God, pray for us sinners, now and at the hour of our death.'

Communal worship, conscious prayer and habitual contemplative prayer can support us so far. However, when pain is excruciating, or our mental-emotional world is in freefall, we can find our whole being taken up with simply enduring the present moment. At such a time, what counts is that prayer of Christ for us at the right hand of God, and the 'groans' too deep for words by which the Spirit also intercedes on our behalf (Rom. 8:26, 34–9; Heb. 4:14–15). This Trinitarian mystery is almost certainly not something consciously felt. Yet beyond all human divisions and rivalries, ideologies and theologies, it is the basis of every form of prayer and prayerfulness, of life in its wholeness, the inexplicable, indestructible core of our being.

Meanwhile for those powerlessly watching a loved one suffer, or passing from this life, or battling to recover life, all we can offer is to be at one, in love, with that unutterable prayer of heaven, which is at once totally personal and for all humanity, hoping and trusting that our very powerlessness might in some way be a conduit of strength and grace.

---

[54] See the thirteenth-century prayer of Richard of Chichester: 'Thanks be to thee, my Lord Jesus Christ, for all the benefits thou hast given me, for all the pains and insults thou hast borne for me. O most merciful redeemer, friend and brother, may I know thee more clearly, love thee more dearly, and follow thee more nearly, day by day. Amen.'

Look, I tell you a mystery! We will not all die, but we will all be changed, in a moment, in the twinkling of an eye, at the last trumpet. For the trumpet will sound, and the dead will be raised imperishable, and we shall be changed. For this perishable thing must clothe itself in imperishability, and this mortal thing clothe itself in immortality. When this perishable body puts on imperishability, and this mortal body puts on immortality, then will the saying that has been written come to pass: "Death has been swallowed up in victory. Where, death, is your victory? Where, death, is your sting?" Now death's sting is sin, and sin's power is the Law; But thanks to God who gives us victory through our Lord Jesus the Anointed. So, my beloved brothers and sisters, be steadfast, immovable, ever abounding in the Lord's work, knowing that in the Lord your labour is not in vain.

(1 Cor. 15:51–8)

SLG PRESS PUBLICATIONS

FP1	*Prayer and the Life of Reconciliation*	Gilbert Shaw (1969)
FP2	*Aloneness not Loneliness*	Mother Mary Clare SLG (1969)
FP4	*Intercession*	Mother Mary Clare SLG (1969)
FP8	*Prayer: Extracts from the Teaching of Father Gilbert Shaw*	Gilbert Shaw (1973)
FP12	*Learning to Pray*	Mother Mary Clare SLG (1970, rev. 3/2025)
FP15	*Death, the Gateway to Life*	Gilbert Shaw (1971, 3/2024)
FP16	*The Victory of the Cross*	Dumitru Stăniloae (1970, 3/2023)
FP26	*The Message of Saint Seraphim*	Irina Gorainov (1974)
FP28	*Julian of Norwich: Four Studies to Commemorate the Sixth Centenary of the Revelations of Divine Love*	Sister Benedicta Ward SLG, Sister Eileen Mary SLG, Sister Mary Paul SLG, A. M. Allchin (1973, 3/2022)
FP43	*The Power of the Name: The Jesus Prayer in Orthodox Spirituality*	Kallistos Ware (1974)
FP46	*Prayer and Contemplation* and *Distractions are for Healing*	Robert Llewelyn (1975, rev. 4/2025)
FP48	*The Wisdom of the Desert Fathers*	trans. Sister Benedicta Ward SLG (1975)
FP50	*Letters of Saint Antony the Great*	trans. Derwas Chitty (1975, 2/2021)
FP54	*From Loneliness to Solitude*	Roland Walls (1976)
FP55	*Theology and Spirituality*	Andrew Louth (1976, rev. 1978, 3/2024)
FP61	*Kabir: The Way of Love and Paradox*	Sister Rosemary SLG (1977)
FP62	*Anselm of Canterbury: A Monastic Scholar*	Sister Benedicta Ward SLG (1973, 2/2024)
FP67	*Mary and the Mystery of the Incarnation: An Essay on the Mother of God in the Theology of Karl Barth*	Andrew Louth (1977, 2/2024)
FP68	*Trinity and Incarnation in Anglican Tradition*	A. M. Allchin (1977, rev. 2/2025)
FP70	*Facing Depression*	Gonville ffrench-Beytagh (1978, 2/2020)
FP71	*The Single Person*	Philip Welsh (1979)
FP72	*The Letters of Ammonas, Successor of St Antony*	trans. Derwas Chitty, introd. Sebastian Brock (1979, 2/2023)
FP74	*George Herbert, Priest and Poet*	Kenneth Mason (1980)
FP75	*A Study of Wisdom: Three Tracts by the Author of The Cloud of Unknowing*	trans. Clifton Wolters (1980)
FP81	*The Psalms: Prayer Book of the Bible*	Dietrich Bonhoeffer, trans. Sister Isabel SLG (1982, rev. 3/2025)
FP82	*Prayer & Holiness: The Icon of Man Renewed in God*	Dumitru Stăniloae (1982, rev. 2/2023)
FP85	*Walter Hilton: Eight Chapters on Perfection & Angels' Song*	trans. Rosemary Dorward (1983, rev. 3/2024)
FP88	*Creative Suffering*	Iulia de Beausobre (1989)
FP90	*Bringing Forth Christ: Five Feasts of the Child Jesus by St Bonaventure*	trans. Eric Doyle OFM (1984, 3/2024)
FP92	*Gentleness in John of the Cross*	Thomas Kane (1985, rev. 2/2025)
FP94	*Saint Gregory Nazianzen: Selected Poems*	trans. John McGuckin (1986, 2/2024)
FP95	*The World of the Desert Fathers: Stories and Sayings from the Anonymous Series of the Apophthegmata Patrum*	trans. Columba Stewart OSB (1986, 2/2020)
FP104	*Growing Old with God*	Timothy N. Rudd (1988, 2/2020)
FP106	*Julian Reconsidered*	Kenneth Leech, Sister Benedicta Ward SLG (1988/ rev. 2/2024)
FP108	*The Unicorn: Meditations on the Love of God*	Harry Galbraith Miller (1989)

FP109	The Creativity of Diminishment	Sister Anke (1990)
FP110	Called to be Priests	Hugh Wybrew (1989, updated 2/2024)
FP111	A Kind of Watershed: An Anglican Lay View of Sacramental Confession	Christine North (1990, updated 2/2022)
FP116	Jesus, the Living Lord	Bishop Michael Ramsey (1992)
FP120	The Monastic Letters of Saint Athanasius the Great	trans. and introd. Leslie Barnard (1994, 2/2023)
FP122	The Hidden Joy	Sister Jane SLG, ed. Dorothy Sutherland (1994)
FP124	Prayer of the Heart: An Approach to Silent Prayer and Prayer in the Night	Alexander Ryrie (1995, 3/2020)
FP126	Evelyn Underhill, Anglican Mystic: Two Centenary Essays	A. M. Allchin, Bishop Michael Ramsey (1977, rev. 4/2025)
FP127	Apostolate and the Mirrors of Paradox	Sydney Evans, ed. Andrew Linzey & Brian Horne (1996)
FP128	The Wisdom of Saint Isaac the Syrian	Sebastian Brock (1997)
FP129	Saint Thérèse of Lisieux: Her Relevance for Today	Sister Eileen Mary SLG (1997)
FP130	Expectations: Five Addresses for Those Beginning Ministry	Sister Edmée SLG (1997, 2/2024)
FP131	Scenes from Animal Life: Fables for the Enneagram Types	Waltraud Kirschke, trans. Sister Isabel SLG (1998)
FP132	Praying the Word of God: The Use of Lectio Divina	Charles Dumont OCSO (1999)
FP133	Love Unknown: Meditations on the Death and Resurrection of Jesus	John Barton (1999, 2/2024)
FP134	The Hidden Way of Love: Jean-Pierre de Caussade's Spirituality of Abandonment	Barry Conaway (1999, rev. 2/2025)
FP135	Shepherd and Servant: The Spiritual Theology of Saint Dunstan	Douglas Dales (2000)
FP137	Pilgrimage of the Heart	Sister Benedicta Ward SLG (2001)
FP138	Mixed Life	Walter Hilton, trans. Rosemary Dorward (2001, enlarged rev. 3/2024)
FP139	In the Footsteps of the Lord: The Teaching of Abba Isaiah of Scetis	John Chryssavgis, Luke Penkett (2001, 2/2023)
FP140	A Great Joy: Reflections on the Meaning of Christmas	Kenneth Mason (2001)
FP141	Bede and the Psalter	Sister Benedicta Ward SLG (2002, 2/2024)
FP142	Abhishiktananda: A Memoir of Dom Henri Le Saux	Murray Rogers, David Barton (2003)
FP143	Friendship in God: The Encounter of Evelyn Underhill & Sorella Maria of Campello	A. M. Allchin (2003, rev. 2/2025)
FP144	Christian Imagination in Poetry and Polity: Some Anglican Voices from Temple to Herbert	Bishop Rowan Williams (2004)
FP145	The Reflections of Abba Zosimas: Monk of the Palestinian Desert	trans. and introd. John Chryssavgis (2005, 3/2022)
FP146	The Gift of Theology: The Trinitarian Vision of Ann Griffiths and Elizabeth of Dijon	A. M. Allchin (2005)
FP147	Sacrifice and Spirit	Bishop Michael Ramsey (2005)
FP148	Saint John Cassian on Prayer	trans. A. M. Casiday (2006, 2/2024)
FP149	Hymns of Saint Ephrem the Syrian	trans. Mary Hansbury (2006, 2/2024)
FP150	Suffering: Why All this Suffering? What Do I Do about It?	Reinhard Körner OCD, trans. Sister Avis Mary SLG (2006)
FP151	A True Easter: The Synod of Whitby 664 AD	Sister Benedicta Ward SLG (2007, 2/2023)
FP152	Prayer as Self-Offering	Alexander Ryrie (2007)
FP153	From Perfection to the Elixir: How George Herbert Fashioned a Famous Poem	Benedick de la Mare (2008, 2/2024)
FP154	The Jesus Prayer: Gospel Soundings	Sister Pauline Margaret CHN (2008)

FP155 *Loving God Whatever: Through the Year with Sister Jane*   Sister Jane SLG (2006)
FP156 *Prayer and Meditation for a Sleepless Night*
                                                    SISTERS OF THE LOVE OF GOD (1993, 3/2024)
FP157 *Being There: Caring for the Bereaved*   John Porter (2009)
FP158 *Learn to Be at Peace: The Practice of Stillness*   Andrew Norman (2010)
FP159 *From Holy Week to Easter*   George Pattison (2010)
FP160 *Strength in Weakness: The Scandal of the Cross*   John W. Rogerson (2010)
FP161 *Augustine Baker: Frontiers of the Spirit*   Victor de Waal (2010, rev. 2/2025)
FP162 *Out of the Depths*
                           Gonville ffrench-Beytagh; epilogue Wendy Robinson (1990, 2/2010)
FP163 *God and Darkness: A Carmelite Perspective*
                                           Gemma Hinricher OCD, trans. Sister Avis Mary SLG (2010)
FP164 *The Gift of Joy*   Curtis Almquist SSJE (2011)
FP165 *'I Have Called You Friends': Suggestions for the Spiritual Life Based on
       the Farewell Discourses of Jesus*   Reinhard Körner OCD (2012)
FP166 *Leisure*   Mother Mary Clare SLG (2012)
FP167 *Carmelite Ascent: An Introduction to Saint Teresa and Saint John of the Cross*
                                                             Mother Mary Clare SLG (1973, rev. 2/2012)
FP168 *Ann Griffiths and Her Writings*   Llewellyn Cumings (2012)
FP169 *The Our Father*   Sister Benedicta Ward SLG (2012)
FP171 *The Spiritual Wisdom of the Syriac Book of Steps*   Robert A. Kitchen (2013)
FP172 *The Prayer of Silence*   Alexander Ryrie (2012)
FP173 *On Tour in Byzantium: Excerpts from The Spiritual Meadow of John Moschus*
                                                             Ralph Martin SSM (2013)
FP174 *Monastic Life*   Bonnie Thurston (2016)
FP175 *Shall All Be Well? Reflections for Holy Week*   Graham Ward (2015)
FP176 *Solitude and Communion: Papers on the Hermit Life*   ed. A. M. Allchin (2015)
FP177 *The Prayers of Jacob of Serugh*   ed. Mary Hansbury (2015)
FP178 *The Monastic Hours of Prayer*   Sister Benedicta Ward SLG (2016)
FP179 *The Desert of the Heart: Daily Readings with the Desert Fathers*
                                                trans. Sister Benedicta Ward SLG (2016)
FP180 *In Company with Christ: Lent, Palm Sunday, Good Friday & Easter to Pentecost*
                                                             Sister Benedicta Ward SLG (2016)
FP181 *Lazarus: Come Out! Reflections on John 11*   Bonnie Thurston (2017)
FP182 *Unknowing & Astonishment: Meditations on Faith for the Long Haul*
                                                             Christopher Scott (2018)
FP183 *Pondering, Praying, Preaching: Romans 8*   Bonnie Thurston (2019, 2/2021)
FP184 *Shem`on the Graceful: Discourse on the Solitary Life*
                                                trans. and introd. Mary Hansbury (2020)
FP185 *God Under My Roof: Celtic Songs and Blessings*   Esther de Waal (2020)
FP186 *Journeying with the Jesus Prayer*   James F. Wellington (2020)
FP187 *Poet of the Word: Re-reading Scripture with Ephraem the Syrian*
                                                             Aelred Partridge OC (2020)
FP188 *Identity and Ritual*   Alan Griffiths (2021)
FP189 *River of the Spirit: The Spirituality of Simon Barrington-Ward*   Andy Lord (2021)
FP190 *Prayer and the Struggle against Evil*   John Barton, Daniel Lloyd,
                                                   James Ramsay, Alexander Ryrie (2021)
FP191 *Dante's Spiritual Journey: A Reading of the Divine Comedy* Tony Dickinson (2021)
FP192 *Jesus the Undistorted Image of God*   John Townroe (2022)
FP193 *Our Deepest Desire: Prayer, Fasting & Almsgiving in the Writings of*

	Saint Augustine of Hippo	Sister Susan SLG (2022)
FP194	Lent with George Herbert	Tony Dickinson (2022)
FP195	Four Ways to the Cross	Tony Dickinson (2022)
FP196	Anselm of Canterbury, Teacher of Prayer	Sister Benedicta Ward SLG (2022)
FP197	With One Heart and Mind: Prayers out of Stillness	Anthony Kemp (2023)
FP198	Sayings of the Urban Fathers & Mothers	James Ashdown (2023)
FP199	Doors	Sister Raphael SLG (2023)
FP200	Monastic Vocation SISTERS OF THE LOVE OF GOD, Bishop Rowan Williams (2021)	
FP201	An Ecology of the Heart: Faith Through the Climate Crisis	Duncan Forbes (2023)
FP202	'In the image of the Image': Gregory of Nyssa's Opposition to Slavery	
		Adam Couchman (2023)
FP203	Gregory of Nyssa and the Sins of Asia Minor	Jonathan Farrugia (2023)
FP204	Discovery	Arthur Bell (2023)
FP205	Living Healing: the Spirituality of Leanne Payne	Andy Lord (2023)
FP206	Still Listening: Sowing the Seeds of the Jesus Prayer	Bruce Batstone CJN (2023)
FP207	Julian of Norwich: Four Essays to Commemorate 650 Years of the	
	Revelations of Divine Love Bishop Graham Usher, Father Colin CSWG,	
	Sister Elizabeth Ruth Obbard OC, Mother Hilary Crupi OJN (2023)	
FP208	TIME	Dumitru Stăniloae, Kallistos Ware (2023)
FP209	Pearls of Life: A Lifebelt for the Spirit	Tony Dickinson (2024)
FP210	The Way and the Truth and the Life: An Exploration by a Follower of the Way	
		James Ramsay (2024)
FP211	Cosmos, Crisis & Christ: Essays of Wendy Robinson	Wendy Robinson (2024)
FP212	Towards a Theology of Psychotherapy: The Spirituality of Wendy Robinson	
		Andrew Louth (2024)
FP213	Immersed in God and the World: Living Priestly Ministry	Andy Lord (2024)
FP214	The Road to Emmaus: A Sculptor's Journey through Time	Rodney Munday (2024)
FP215	Prayer Too Deep for Words	Sister Edmée SLG (2024)
FP216	The Prayers of St Isaac of Nineveh	Sebastian Brock (2024)
FP217	Two Medieval English Saints: Cuthbert and Alban	Sister Benedicta Ward SLG (2024)
FP218	Encountering the Depths	Mother Mary Clare SLG (1981, rev. 3/2024)
FP219	Conflict and Concord Sister Susan SLG, Bishop Humphrey Southern,	
	Bronwen Neil, Sister Rosemary SLG, Sister Clare-Louise SLG (2024)	
FP220	Divine Love in the Song of Songs	Sister Edmée SLG (2024)
FP221	Zeal for the Faith: An Introduction to Christian-Muslim Dialogue Tony Dickinson (2024)	
FP222	Bernard & Abelard	Sister Edmée SLG (2024)
FP223	Eliot's Transitions: T. S. Eliot's Search for Identity and the Society	
	of the Sacred Mission at Kelham Hall	Vincent Strudwick (2024)
FP224	Landscape, Soul and Spirit: Ecology, Prayer and Robert Macfarlane	Andy Lord (2025)
FP225	Our Home is in God	John Townroe (2025)
FP226	Signs of the Times: A Brief Survey of the Bible's Apocalyptic Writings Tony Dickinson (2025)	
FP227	And We Shall be Changed: Christian Reflections on Death and Dying James Ramsay (2025)	
FP228	Journeys into the Bible	Sister Edmée SLG (2025)
FP226	Directions	Sister Edmée SLG (2025)

www.slgpress.co.uk

CONTEMPLATIVE POETRY SERIES

CP1	*Amado Nervo: Poems of Faith and Doubt*	trans. John Gallas (2021)
CP2	*Anglo-Saxon Poets: The High Roof of Heaven*	trans. John Gallas (2021)
CP3	*Middle English Poets: Where Grace Grows Ever Green*	ed. John Gallas (2021)
CP4	*The Voice inside Our Home: Selected Poems*	Edward Clarke (2022)
CP5	*Women & God: Drops in the Sea of Time*	trans. and ed. John Gallas (2022)
CP6	*Gabrielle de Coignard & Vittoria Colonna: Fly Not Too High*	trans. John Gallas (2022)
CP7	*Chancing on Sanctity: Selected Poems*	James Ramsay (2022)
CP8	*Gabriela Mistral: This Far Place*	trans. John Gallas (2023)
CP9	*Henry Vaughan & George Herbert: Divine Themes and Celestial Praise*	ed. Edward Clarke (2023)
CP10	*Love Will Come with Fire: Anthology*	SISTERS OF THE LOVE OF GOD (2023)
CP11	*Touchpapers: Anthology*	coll. and trans. John Gallas (2023)
CP12	*Seasons of my Soul: Selected Poems*	Clare McKerron (2023)
CP13	*Reinhard Sorge: Take Flight to God*	trans. John Gallas (2024)
CP14	*Embertide: Encountering Saint Frideswide*	Romola Parish (2024)
CP15	*Thomas Campion: Made All of Light*	ed. and introd. Julia Craig-McFeely (2024)
CP16	*When God Hides: Selected Poems*	Joseph Evans (2025)

VESTRY GUIDES

VG1	*The Visiting Minister: How to Welcome Visiting Clergy to Your Church*	Paul Monk (2021)
VG2	*Help! No Minister! or Please Take the Service*	Paul Monk (2022)
VG3	*The Liturgy of the Eucharist: An Introductory Guide*	Paul Monk (2024)

www.slgpress.co.uk

The Sisters of the Love of God is an Anglican community of women religious living a contemplative monastic life.

To learn more about the Community and the Convent of the Incarnation at Fairacres, Oxford, see our website www.slg.org.uk.

As well as supporting those seeking to follow a vocation to the monastic life, the Community has a number of forms of association for those who feel drawn to share in the Sisters' life of prayer: Fellowship of the Love of God, Companions, Priests Associate or Oblate Sisters.

For more information email sisters@slg.org.uk or write to The Reverend Mother, Convent of the Incarnation, Parker Street, Oxford, OX4 1TB, UK.